The Gospel According to Josie

Margaret —
Enjoy these stories
about the ups & the
downs of life with my special
pooch & hunting partner! God bless you.

The Gospel According to Josie

The Bond Between a Man and His Hunting Dog

PJ Sanders

ISBN: 1515388352
ISBN 13: 9781515388357
Library of Congress Control Number: 2015912816
CreateSpace Independent Publishing Platform
North Charleston, South Carolina

Preface & Acknowledgements

Josie is a purebred German Wirehaired Pointer. The stories in this book are all true and span fourteen years, from the time Josie was born to well into her golden years.

There are several women to whom I owe a sincere debt of gratitude, not only for the creation of this book, but for bringing Josie into my life in the first place. Sandra Hoesel is the owner of SandStorm Kennels, and owned Josie's daddy, Boise. Sandy spent many, many hours teaching me to train Josie to find birds, hold point, and retrieve. She was a great teacher and mentor, without whom there would not have been a Josie, much less a *Gospel According to Josie.*

A heartfelt note of appreciation is also extended to Carla German, my sister-in-law, who proofread and edited all of these stories. She offered suggestions for clarification and smooth transition throughout the tales. Her diligence and attention to detail are most appreciated.

All of the sketches in *The Gospel According to Josie* are original drawings, crafted specifically for this book. The same is true for the cover sketch. Sasha Miller has poured her amazing artistic talent as well as her heart into the drawings that grace the pages of this book. I am deeply grateful for her devotion to getting everything just right every time. It was truly a pleasure to work with her on this project.

My wife, Cindy, has been a big part of Josie's life from day one. She has put up with Josie's nose prints all over the patio doors for all these years, as well as muddy dog tracks on freshly scrubbed floors and the emergency trips to the vet or animal hospital in the middle of the night. There have been "accidents" on the floor on too many occasions. She has taken such good care of Josie when I was not at home. Yes, Josie is a shedder, so there is dog hair here, there, everywhere! Cindy has demonstrated the patience of a saint time and again, through all of the ups and downs of life with Josie.

Josie - Table of Contents

1

In the Beginning

Haar Baron's Patchwork Josie was born on April 9, 2001, in a litter of eight purebred German Wirehaired Pointer puppies sired by FC, Master Hunter CH Flatlander's Boise CD MH who was owned by Sandra Hoesel of SandStorm Kennels fame. The FC stands for Field Champion and the MH for Master Hunter which signifies a highly trained and decorated stud dog. The dam - mother - is also a decorated dog, though not owning as many letters of the alphabet as the sire! The bottom line is that Josie comes from great hunting stock.

The "Patchwork" in her name is in remembrance of my first dog, a Brittany named Patches, whom I got as a puppy about four years earlier. When he was just two years old, shortly after earning his Junior Hunter certification through AKC-sanctioned hunt tests, I took Patches on my first-ever pheasant hunt to North Dakota. The trip turned from anticipation and excitement to tragedy when another hunter - not part of our hunting party - intentionally shot Patches - twice - killing him. When we confronted the man, he initially denied even seeing my dog but later admitted what he had done and brought us to where he hid the body. The grief I experienced that day was awful. I will never forget calling my wife Cindy to tell her and our two sons that I would not be bringing Patches home with me. We buried him on a windswept butte overlooking the field where he died.

I may never understand, this side of heaven, how God provided a way for me to forgive the man who committed this despicable deed, but He did, and in time, I have come not only to forgive him - though he has never asked for forgiveness or even apologized for what he did - but also to pray for him and his family; that the Lord would soften his heart, for I could not imagine what his life must be like, that he could so easily shoot and kill another man's dog and then lie about it - all with seemingly no remorse.

Life with Patches was over, and about eighteen months later, life with Josie would begin.

My wife, Cindy, and I talked for a long time about getting another dog. I decided I would like a dog that was a little hardier and bigger than Patches, a dog more suited to waterfowling and retrieving ducks in the frigid waters of a Wisconsin November. Thus, I decided to get a

German Wirehaired Pointer. I have always believed that pointing dogs were much more fun to hunt with than flushers, and the fuzzy-faced Wires were just the ticket. I wanted a dog with a ticked coat - grey hair blended in with brown. A female this time, not to breed, but a dog with more of a motherly personality.

So it was that I found Sandstorm Kennels online and learned more about the breed and the planned litter of puppies that would be whelped in spring. I put down my deposit, and shortly after the puppies were born, I drove down to Illinois to pick out the one I wanted. I knew which one I wanted as soon as I saw her - her eyes were still closed, but she was colored with a beautifully ticked coat with a couple of brown spots and a mostly brown head. My son, Jesse, and I returned to Illinois when the puppies were eight weeks old and brought Josie into our home and into our hearts!

I will always be grateful to Sandy Hoesel, owner of Sandstorm Kennels and Josie's dad, Boisy, for the hours and hours they committed to helping me learn how to train Josie to find birds, hold the point, and then make the retrieve. The weeks of training became months and then a year. It was certainly a proud day when Josie received her fourth blue ribbon from the American Kennel Club and was officially acknowledged as an AKC Junior Hunter.

The stories in this book are a collection of adventures and misadventures that have occurred over the years as Josie and I have gone afield and afloat together on our hunting trips in not only our home state of Wisconsin but also in North and South Dakota, Iowa and Arkansas.

The 2000 goose hunting season was the year in between Patches and Josie, but my son Benjamin and I had a pretty good year. The Department of Natural Resources issued six tags per hunter for those of us choosing to hunt in the fabled Horicon Zone in central Wisconsin.

Ben and I spent some time hunting from blinds located near the northern boundary of the refuge. The geese coming into and leaving the zone numbered in the thousands, but most of these birds flew safely out of gunshot range, high overhead. Ben and I did, however, have some good fortune and filled a couple of tags together while hunting along the refuge border. I went back to the blinds on another occasion and managed to fill two more of my tags.

So it was that the last day of the season found Ben and me paddling our duck skiff along the Rock River in the Theresa Marsh with hopes of filling a couple of our last tags. DNR regulations stipulated that only two geese could be taken each day by a hunter. I only had two tags left, and Ben had four. So we were hopeful of each taking two geese to wrap up the season.

We arrived at the boat landing in Theresa and quickly got the skiff in the water, loaded in our gear and pushed off for the fifteen-minute paddle that would take us to the bend in the river where we had permission to hunt. We set out the four floating decoys about twenty yards from shore and pulled the skiff in among the reeds. We had only been set up for a few minutes when a group of three geese circled wide around the decoys and landed in the river near the far bank, sixty yards or more from where we were hidden among the cattails. Excitedly, we watched and waited, as the three swimming geese slowly worked their way toward our small spread of decoys. I fought the urge to give a soft call on my goose call which hung around my neck on a lanyard. As long as they were coming our way, better not to mess things up by blowing too loudly and scaring them off.

When at last the geese were almost to the outside edge of the decoys, I whispered to Ben that I thought they were close enough to shoot. I don't like ground-swatting birds so I told him we would jump up, and when the birds took to the air, we would fire. I whispered, "Ready, go!"

We jumped to our feet. Immediately the big birds leapt from the water and became airborne. We started shooting, the gunshots drowning out the honking as massive wings lifted the Canada geese upward. The two geese on the outside of the trio fell back to the water, while the middle goose made good its escape. Ben and I gave each other an excited hug and pushed the skiff out into the river to retrieve the two fallen geese. Hearing a lonely honk, we were startled to see the third goose flying back towards the decoys. It made a solitary pass over the downed geese floating in the water just outside of the decoys. The lone survivor seemed to look back for one last glance then flew off. Neither of us even raised our gun as we watched the bird disappear out of sight.

In the span of ten minutes we retrieved the two geese, tagged them, and were back in hiding along the shore of the river. We talked quietly about the return of the third goose while we watched and listened. The sun began to slip from the sky, indicating only about twenty minutes until the day - and the season - would be over. A gentle breeze stirred the decoys as they lay in the shallow water, tethered to their anchors.

A distant honk-honking of a pair of geese winging their way towards us brought my goose call to my lips. The pair readily responded and swung towards us as we crouched in the skiff, concealing ourselves from their watchful, wary eyes. As the birds circled ever more closely, I whispered to Ben that we would take them on the next pass. They came around into the wind, wings cupped, necks outstretched, landing gear down. "Take 'em!" I shouted, and we jumped to our feet. Both geese tumbled into the water at the sound of our guns. I put my arm around Ben's shoulder and congratulated him for his fine shooting. We stood in the skiff as the sun - which painted the clouds a brilliant orange - dropped from the western sky. We shared a brief prayer of thanksgiving for the Lord's bounty this afternoon, even more, for the beauty and the opportunity we had to spend this time together. As we prepared to push the skiff back into the river to pick up the geese and our decoys, Ben pointed to our little spread. Two of the decoys had spun around so that they were beak-to-beak, their heads and necks forming a perfect heart, a fitting symbol of the love and affection shared that afternoon in the marsh.

2

Men's Retreat

PLANS WERE BEING finalized for a men's retreat for the guys at our church, Crossway Church, which is part of the Christian and Missionary Alliance. We would be heading over to Village Creek Bible Camp in Lansing, Iowa, which is just across the Mississippi River from Wisconsin. I was asked to deliver one of the talks to the fifty men who would be in attendance.

My talk at the retreat would be the genesis for the idea of "The Gospel According to Josie," as I was asked to talk with the men about their relationships with God. My own beliefs about God revolve around the fact that He truly desires for us to spend time with Him, whether in prayer, song, devotion or quiet conversation in the silence of our heart. I know that He will pursue us, actively seek us out, provide opportunities for us to reach out to take His hand which is always extended, waiting patiently for us to take hold of it. The well-known Bible verse found in the Book of Revelation says it this way: "Behold I stand at the door and knock. Whoever opens the door, I will come in and eat with him." These words serve as an invitation to all who are seeking, to all who are curious, to all who have lost our way. An invitation to open the door to our heart and our life and to invite Him in.

The idea of tying my relationship with my German Wirehaired Pointer, Josie, into my talk at the retreat was solidified when I considered how much Josie loves to be with me and will pursue me when I am not paying attention to her. If she is in the house when I get home, she comes running as soon as the back door opens. There she is, her little bobbed tail wagging wildly, eager to give me a kiss that seems to say, "I'm so glad you're home. Let's spend some time together. We can play or go for a walk or play fetch. As long as we are together, it really doesn't matter what we are doing. I just want to be with you." I believe that God Our Father desires to spend time with each of His children - and we are all His children - whether in song, Bible study, prayer, contemplation or reflection.

Josie will follow me from room to room, upstairs and downstairs. She just wants to be with me; she wants me to pay attention to her and to acknowledge her presence and importance in my life. Whenever I go outside, Josie wants to come outside, too. She will usually lie in the grass while I am cutting the lawn, but when I move to another side of the house, she will get up and come over to that side too. She desires to be able to see me all the time. Oftentimes, in the middle of the night,

I am awakened by the clicking sound of Josie's nails on the tiles in the hallway as she pads down to our bedroom door where she will peer in to make sure I am still there. Satisfied, she will walk back down the hallway to her bed in the dining room and go back to sleep. In the same way, God wants to spend time with his children, and since He has breathed life into each and every one of us, we are, indeed, His children. He demonstrated the profound depths of that love when He sent His son Jesus to earth as the atoning sacrifice for all of our failings and sins.

I also spoke to the men about God's unconditional love for us. Our heavenly Father loves us regardless of how we act towards Him or to each other. Good thing. We cannot earn our way into heaven. We simply cannot be good enough. The Bible, which includes all of life's instructions, says, in many places, that our eternal salvation is simply a matter of faith. It's that easy. The apostle Paul perhaps said it best in the Book of Ephesians where he penned the words: "For it is by grace you have been saved, through faith, and this is not from yourselves, it is the gift of God; not by works, so that no one can boast." I shared with the men at the retreat that my interactions with Josie were a daily reminder of that unconditional love which is intertwined with God's forgiving heart because she never keeps track of the times I mess up, like forgetting to give her fresh water, waiting too long to clip her nails, running her when it is too hot, cutting our walks too short, or being late with her supper. Thankfully, Josie is also forgiving when it comes to miscues and mistakes afield such as my getting lost, not bringing enough food/water along on a hunt, and oh my - missing birds that she worked so hard to find! On this last point, however, Josie has, on more than one occasion, rolled her eyes when I missed a shot on a bird that she worked so hard to find and then go point for me. But she does not keep track of my wrongs; neither does God. Lastly, in the Book of Matthew, we are commanded to love our neighbor as we love ourself. Josie excels at loving everybody! She is pretty sure that everybody needs a doggy kiss from her, too. She is a reminder of God's love for us, too.

So it was, that the title of my talk at the retreat has also become the title of this book - *The Gospel According to Josie.* For fourteen years now, Josie has served a constant reminder of God's love for us and His forgiveness towards us. He desires to have a relationship with us and to spend time with us every day. I do find myself wondering, however, if others see the traits of God in me, as I have seen them in my dog. I still have some work to do...

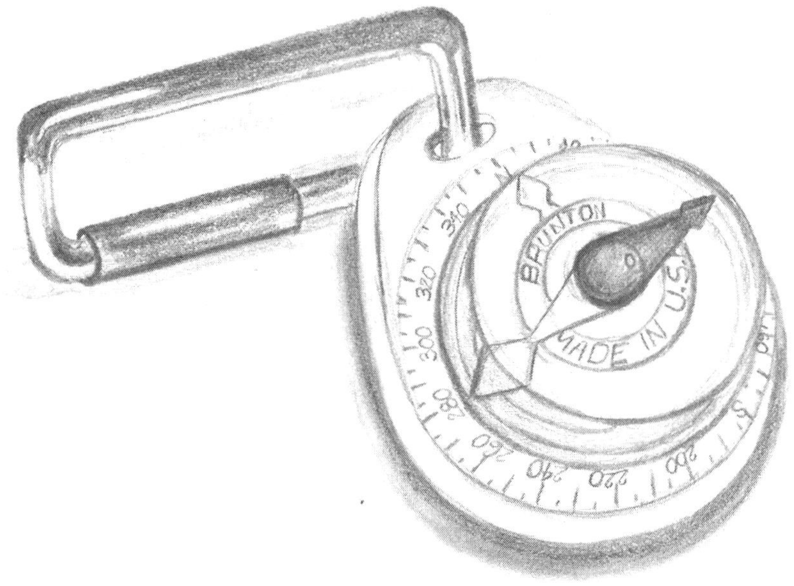

3

Polar Bear Plunge

One of the best things about cottontail rabbit hunting in Wisconsin is the fact that the season runs all the way through the end of February. That's long after ducks and geese and grouse have closed for the year. So it was, on a frigid Saturday morning in the middle of February, that Josie and I found ourselves on a bunny hunt in the Allenton Marsh. I figured that the six inches or so of snow that blanketed the ground would put both sighting and tracking rabbits in my favor.

A few years earlier, on a pheasant hunt in North Dakota, Josie had begun to point rabbits in much the same way that she points pheasants. While the rabbits oftentimes did not sit very tight for her, the times they did made for some pretty good shooting, and as we worked our way slowly through the marsh, good shooting was what I was anticipating.

Because the mercury hovered in the single digits on this particular day, Josie was sporting a set of blaze-orange booties to keep the snow from freezing between her toes. We worked our way down through the stand of oaks and navigated the north end of the swamp where rabbits were to be found from time to time - but not today. There were not even many fresh tracks. Perhaps because of the cold temperatures, the bunnies were hunkered down in their burrows. In warmer weather, this swamp was very difficult to navigate, with knee-deep water in some places and sticky muck in pretty much all of the places. Today, however, with everything frozen solid, the walking was pretty easy. The cattails and bulrushes were crackling and snapping as we passed through them.

I decided we would meander over to another part of the property along the power lines where the cover was not as thick. A quick peek at my compass assured me that I was headed in the right direction, although there was not much chance of getting lost, as the marsh was not all that big, and I had been there many times.

A fairly deep creek ran through the marsh in this area and was now covered with snow. The cold temperatures would have created a safe layer of ice allowing for safe crossing of the creek - or so I thought! I heard the crash of ice breaking followed by a sudden yelp from Josie and spun around to see that she had broken through the ice that covered the creek. The thought struck me too late that the water in the creek was moving fast enough to keep from freezing very solid, and the blanket of snow had served more as an insulator from the cold than as a chilling factor that would aid in the forming of ice. Josie had almost made it over to the far side of the creek before her sixty pounds broke through the thin crust of ice. Only her fuzzy little face and two orange-clad front feet were visible as the rest of her body was submerged in the freezing water. I could not bear to think of what would happen if she lost her grip on the edge of the hole and dropped beneath the surface. I could see right away that I would not be able to reach her from my side of the creek, and I certainly could not walk out to get her. Two steps onto the ice, and I would break through as well, and I didn't know if the water would be over my head or not. "Hold on, girl. I'll get you out. Hold on." A large tree had fallen across the creek about sixty feet from where Josie had broken through. I raced towards the makeshift bridge - snow covered and slippery as it would be - while keeping an eye on my dog over my shoulder, praying that God would keep her safe until I could get to her.

Upon reaching the fallen tree, I could see that it was big enough to hold my weight if only I could cross the twenty feet without slipping off and dropping into the creek myself. I carefully stepped up onto the log, thankful that there were few branches that had to be navigated. As I gingerly inched my way across, I kept calling out to Josie, assuring her that I was coming, that she needed to hang on. I could see that she was struggling to get herself up out of the hole, but to no avail. Her hind feet were well off of the bottom of the creek, and there was nothing for her to push off of to get herself out. As I stepped off the log onto Josie's side of the creek and started to run back to her, I could see that she was now shivering, her big brown eyes pleading with me to hurry up. I could hear her whimpering as I got close to where she had fallen through the ice.

Josie was only about five feet from where I now stood on the edge of the creek but still too far to reach from shore. My plan was for me to only step with one foot onto the ice which I knew would immediately give way but to try to keep my other foot on the snowy bank so I could get both of us back out. Bracing for the cold, but still fearing Josie might slip beneath the ice at any second, I took the step onto the ice that would get me within reach of my pooch. Instantly, the ice broke, and I was balancing on one foot, the freezing water above my knee and well above the top of my hunting boot. I managed to reach far enough to grab Josie's collar and then shifted my weight back towards the foot still on land. A couple of sloshy hops, and I was able to pull my shivering dog up onto the bank next to me. Josie gave a watery shake. She was shivering uncontrollably now. Quickly, I undid the velcro straps that held the booties on Josie's feet as they were filled with water and stuffed them into my pocket. I peeled off my hunting jacket, wrapped her in it and picked her up. With my shotgun slung over my shoulder, and my soggy dog safe in my arms, I started back towards the truck, figuring that it was only twenty minutes away. I thanked God for sparing the life of my four-legged hunting partner and asked Him to continue to watch over us during our trek back to the truck. The left leg of my hunting pants had already frozen solid and my soggy foot was already very cold.

After ten minutes, I realized I would not be able to carry Josie all the way back to the truck - her sixty pounds feeling like one hundred sixty! Maybe if she were walking, she would generate more internal body heat. I didn't know, but my arms were aching, and I had to set her down in the snow. I pulled my wet jacket back on and urged Josie to hurry along with me. Without her booties and her feet wet, she had ice forming between her toes in less than a minute and sat down in the snow - unwilling to walk any further. She looked so pitiful - shaking and shivering, little icicles beginning form on her coat. I slipped my jacket off again, wrapped her in it, and then scooped her back up into my arms. I trudged on towards the truck, having to stop every couple of minutes to rest. I would sit in the snow with Josie still on my lap, resting my arms while I held her close to keep her warm.

The twenty-minute walk back to the truck took closer to forty, but I was so grateful to finally set Josie on the front seat. I started the engine and switched the heater on. In less than ten minutes the truck began to get nice and warm. Josie had stopped shaking, and the icicles that had hung from her beard had begun to melt. As we drove home to a warm bed for her and a hot shower for me, I thanked God once again for delivering us to safety!

4

Morning Walks

Josie and I start each day together with a morning walk. Before heading out, I give her a dose of glucosamine and chondroitin to ease stiffness and discomfort in her hips and joints. She will simply not open her mouth to take the pill nor will she allow me to slip the pill into a small piece of bread smeared with peanut butter or jam as she will take the piece of bread in her mouth and work the pill out from between the two little pieces of bread and spit it out onto the ground. I have had to resort to grinding the pill into a powder and then sprinkling the powder onto the peanut butter and then making a mini sandwich with another small piece of bread. This sandwich she will gobble down in a single bite hardly bothering to chew.

Josie is a creature of habit and will not venture out on our walk unless she has something to carry in her mouth. I'm not sure just when this became a mandatory part of our morning walks, but it has been going on for years. It probably began in her early years when she was quite fond of carrying little stuffed animals around the house. It was a small step to carrying them outside, and then we'd be on our way. The problem is that our walks through the field and woods at the end of the street is "off leash," so I could never tell where she would drop the toy. It wasn't long before all of her toys were somewhere out in the field never again to be seen.

Cindy and I hit upon a novel solution while vacationing in Canada one summer. We stopped at a place where they raised sheep and sold goods made from sheepskin such as moccasins, gloves, and jackets. They also sold bags of leather scraps that still had the wool on. We came to call these scraps "fluffies." Josie was thrilled with them and would not leave the garage each morning until she had one in her mouth.

She also will not come out the back door until she walks once around the dining room table - in a clockwise direction. I would have my boots and jacket on, give her something to carry in her mouth, and then she would walk once around the table before stepping out of the house.

Once she had taken her meds and had her fluffy in her mouth, we could head out to the field for our walk. Well, not quite. Another "must do first" for Josie was to trot over to the two-storm sewer grates located on either side of the street and give them each a good sniff and a stare, all while she had something in her mouth. Only once did I ever see a raccoon scurry down one of those grates, but for some reason, they hold a particular fascination for her.

The field at the end of our street where we go for our walks butts up against some woods which adjoins more fields and more woods. On some days, our stroll may be as brief as fifteen minutes. Other mornings, when we have a little more time, we may wander through the woods and fields for an hour-and-a-half or more. There are all sorts of wildlife sightings on our morning walks though we do not see critters every morning. We do come across white-tailed deer, ducks, squirrels, raccoons, coyotes and rabbits. The most engaging of all, however, are the turkeys. Josie will get "birdy" when she gets a snootful of scent. Her little tail starts going a hundred miles an hour. With her nose to the ground, she follows the trail of the big bird. Oftentimes, the turkey will burst from the cover of the tall grasses with its thunderous pounding of wings drowning out the soft clucking as it becomes airborne. As much fun as it is when we come across an adult turkey, it is really exciting when we come across a hen with a brood of young'ens in the springtime. On one particular spring morning walk, we chanced upon a hen that was reluctant to fly or run away which aroused my suspicions. Peering intently into the grass along the side of the path, I spotted several baby turkeys no bigger than robins. They were much too young to fly - barely old enough even to walk. It was no easy task getting Josie away from them! Another time we came across an older brood with young birds that were just learning to fly. Josie could not decide which one to chase first as there must have been a dozen small birds running away and then taking wing. As soon as one bird flew off, Josie would race back to where the others were still on the ground. She'd sniff out another one, and the chase was on again. It always ended with the bird escaping through the air, but for Josie, the joy was in the chase, not necessarily in the catch.

Another favorite side trip on our morning walks is a stop at the retention pond by the bank, which is located at the end of a dead-end road and not really out of the way for us to stop off during our morning walks. There is an aerator that sprays water into the air as an anti-mosquito device, but it was a perfect place to lap up some water or, on really warm days, go for a little swim - Josie, not me!

Once we emerge from the field and are back on the street for the short walk back home, Josie engages in one final ritual on our morning walks. She leans down so that her head is on the asphalt and rubs her chin back and forth - the asphalt scratching her bearded chin.

This has been our ritual for us to start our day together for over fourteen years.

5

Man Overboard

Where the Bark River passes through southern Washington County is really more like a wide stream than a river. In most places, it varies between twenty and thirty feet across. It is mostly too shallow to run a boat with a motor, even a Jon boat with a little 9.9 Merc. But it is a fine place to paddle a duck skiff which is what Josie and I found ourselves doing on a frigid November Saturday morning some years ago. The temperature was in the low twenties. Ice was forming along the edges of the river.

I backed the pickup truck down to the edge of the water as dawn was breaking. Josie, as usual, was very excited to get the show on the road. She was whimpering and shaking in her crate which was safely strapped to the inside of the truck under the protective cap. After donning my waders, I unstrapped the skiff and eased the nose of the boat into the black, icy water. By now Josie was really working herself into a lather because she was so anxious to get on with our duck hunt. I quickly loaded the rest of the gear into the skiff - shotgun, shooting box, life jacket, paddle and a bag of decoys. After securing the skiff to the shore next to the landing, I found a spot to park the truck and let Josie out of her crate. We hurried to the water's edge. Carefully, I stepped into the middle of the bottom of the skiff, keeping my weight centered and as low as possible to prevent the tipping of my little watercraft. I motioned for her to jump in behind me, and we pushed off. I turned the skiff north, and we were on our way towards Bark Lake, some two miles upriver, just as legal shooting time arrived. Our timing was perfect. I could jump shoot as I paddled up to the lake. Once there, we would throw out the decoys and hunt from the cover of the cattails for a couple of hours, then jump shoot back downstream to the landing. I could not imagine a better way to spend a morning.

My shotgun was loaded and at the ready and was resting on the wooden camo box that also held a couple of boxes of shells, a compass, extra gloves, a sandwich and a thermos of coffee. I knelt as I paddled, stroking quietly and slowly, expecting a startled duck to take wing around every bend in the river.

Even though it was a cold morning, the day was beautiful - a little windy with mostly sunny skies. In the first fifteen or twenty minutes of paddling, we had not seen any ducks, although we did paddle past a couple of hunters who had set out a dozen or so decoys and were hunkered down in the bulrushes on the edge of the river. We acknowledged each other with a silent nod. Josie seemed like she would liked to have stopped and get to know their dog a little better, but I paddled on, ignoring her whimpering. She was confined to a small space behind me in the skiff. She had room to move from side to side of the skiff, but that was all. The less room she had to roam around in the boat, the less chance she had of causing any problems.

We continued on our slow journey, hugging the shore on each turn, using the contour of the river to keep us hidden from the watchful eyes of any waterfowl that we might come across until we were within range. I was thoroughly enjoying myself, keeping one eye on the water ahead and the other cast skyward. Movement overhead caught my attention, as a pair of mallards winged their way across the sky, flying from left to right. The ducks were too high for a shot, but not too high for Josie to see them! As they crossed over above me, Josie suddenly shifted from the port side to the starboard so she could keep a close eye on them too. In her excitement, she got her front paws up on the gunwale which was just enough sudden shifting of her sixty pounds to cause the skiff to list a little too far to the starboard, and everything and everybody was dumped from the skiff into the frigid water! It happened so quickly that I could hardly believe that one second I was glancing at the ducks overhead, and the next I was underwater, gasping to catch a breath of air! The only good news was that the water was only about four-feet deep so there was not any real danger of my drowning, as I was able to regain my footing - now standing chest deep next to the half-filled skiff. Nearby, my life jacket floated uselessly, bobbing in the water next to the wooden shooting box which, unfortunately, now devoid of its contents of the boxes of shells and the thermos which were now resting somewhere on the bottom of the river, along with my shotgun. The paddle was floating closely by as was the bag of decoys. Josie, in the meantime, had swum over to the shore, climbed up onto the bank and stood looking at me with an expression that seemed to say, "Wow, that was really an unexpected turn of events, huh?" Water dripped from her beard.

The bottom of the river was surprisingly firm, and I could shuffle around until I could feel my shotgun with my feet. I was able to work one foot under the firearm, and holding onto the skiff for balance, I was able to raise the muzzle of the gun up high enough to where I could reach down and grab it with my hand. I raised it up high enough to watch the water drain from the barrel and receiver, then with the skiff in tow, sloshed over to where Josie stood on dry land! After retrieving the life jacket, paddle, decoys and box, I pulled the skiff up far enough to tip it on its side to drain the water. Only then did I realize how terribly cold I was as I was soaked from about the waist up. My neoprene waders provided a pretty water-tight seal around my upper body so there was not a lot of water inside the waders, but my top half was soaked to the skin, and I was shivering uncontrollably.

I quickly placed the box back in the boat, set the shotgun in the holders on the box, tossed the lifejacket on the floor, dropped in the decoys and lowered myself back into the skiff, clutching the paddle in my shaking hands. I signaled for Josie to get back in behind me, and I started paddling back to the boat landing, not nearly so slowly or quietly this time!

The nose of the skiff nudged the bank of the river at the landing about twenty minutes later. Still shaking from the cold, I struggled to my feet and climbed out. Josie was right on my heels, seemingly wondering why our adventure was coming to an end so quickly. With some difficulty, I was able to get my keys out of my pocket, thankful that they did not end up at the bottom of the drink. I got Josie in the front seat and backed the truck back down to the water's edge where I was able to slide the skiff back into the bed of the pickup. Five minutes later, with the skiff securely tied down, and the items I was able to retrieve from the river packed in the back of the truck, I started the truck and headed for home, the heater on full blast, Josie sitting in the passenger seat next to me, ready for our next adventure.

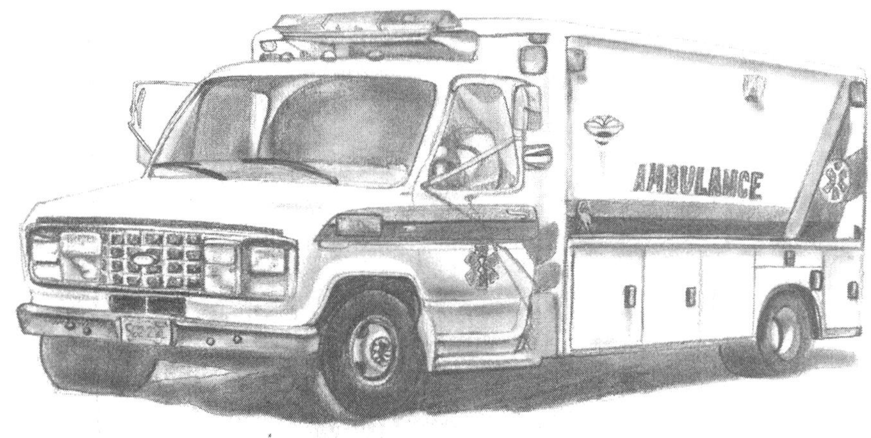

6

Brush With Death

When Josie was about a year old, my wife, Cindy, and I travelled up to my home town of De Pere, Wisconsin, to visit my folks for a weekend. We decided to bring Josie with us since she was still so young. We had not yet found a kennel in which to board her, so that was another reason to bring her on the road trip. Josie did not particularly like being crated in the basement all by herself for the night, and her early morning barking woke me from a sound sleep. Not wanting everybody else in the house to be awakened as well, I quickly dressed and hurried downstairs.

I was using an electronic training collar with Josie, so I fastened it on her neck, slipped the transmitter into my pocket and ducked out the back door of the house. My parents' home is only about a hundred yards from a set of railroad tracks, and that seemed like a good place to walk Josie that morning. It only took a few minutes to get there. Then we headed south along the tracks. There were plenty of wonderful distractions for Josie to enjoy along the tracks - rabbits, frogs and all sorts of smells that only a dog could love! We meandered along for about an hour and then turned around to head back. Seeking a little different experience for the return trip, Josie and I left the tracks and headed toward the more open spaces of the practice field for the St. Norbert College football team.

I knew that the field would be deserted at that time on a Saturday morning so we pretty much had the place to ourselves - except for a gray squirrel that came scampering out in front of Josie as we neared the street. Josie took off after the bushy tail, ignoring my hollering and whistling for her to stop. As the squirrel neared the street, I grabbed the transmitter, quickly dialed up the highest setting and hit the button to get Josie to stop. This highest setting usually resulted in a yelp from Josie, but only a slight flinch registered as she tore across the street in hot pursuit of the squirrel which made it to safety on the other side of the street when it scurried up a tree. I was still pressing the transmitter button and still hollering for Josie as I ran toward the street. Josie finally turned to come back across the street right into the path of an oncoming car. The sound of screeching brakes was followed by the sickening sound of my little dog being hit by the front bumper of the car. A sudden flashback brought the death of my Brittany Patches to mind. I could not imagine having two dogs killed within such a short time of each other. I was also struck by the irony of the fact that I had been hit by a car when I was only five years old on this very street - a quarter mile further north. A broken clavicle earned me an ambulance ride to St. Vincent's Hospital in Green Bay. Also a tragedy narrowly averted.

Josie lay in the middle of the road, alive, but unable to stand. I could not tell how badly she was hurt, but she did not seem to be bleeding. The driver of the car that hit her stopped and got out of his car. I rushed to Josie and tried to calm her without moving her for fear of doing even more damage. As I knelt in the road trying to decide what to do, I was aware of another vehicle approaching the accident site. I glanced up to see an ambulance braking to a stop only a few yards from where I was cradling Josie's head in the middle of the road. A squad car pulled up behind the ambulance, lights flashing to warn other drivers of our presence.

The two EMT's got out of the ambulance and rushed over to us. I told them what happened and that I was staying at my parents' home about six blocks away. They got a blanket out of their ambulance, wrapped Josie up, then carried her to the ambulance where they had me sit in the back and placed the injured dog on my lap. They then proceeded to drive me to my folks' home. They refused to take anything for their trouble. They did not bill me. They just came to my rescue when I was in desperate need of emergency medical assistance.

I carried Josie into the house and relayed the events of the morning. Dad found the address for the animal emergency clinic in Green Bay, and we were off. Josie whimpered in my arms most of the twenty-minute trip. After Josie was examined, I learned that she did not have any broken bones, but she did have a collapsed lung and multiple bruises and lacerations. They would need to keep her overnight to be sure that no infections developed, and they were optimistic about being able to successfully repair her lung. So, with a mixture of relief and sadness, we left Josie at the clinic overnight.

Returning to the animal hospital the next day, the attendants brought Josie out to us. In order to properly clean each of the abrasions, they shaved Josie's fur down to the hide. There were six or seven such shavings, and a few of them had required stitches to close the gash. She looked like she had been caught in a giant blender. The veterinarian told me how lucky Josie was to be alive and not to have suffered anything more severe than a collapsed lung, though that was no small problem either. Armed with a bottle of antibiotics and a bottle of pain pills, Dad and I left the hospital, carrying my little banged-up dog in my arms, her soft brown eyes telling me that it was okay; she would be fine. A tear rolled down my cheek and landed on the top of her head.

A couple of weeks later and a visit to my own vet for a re-check found Josie on the mend. Her lung had re-inflated, all of the cuts were healing, and the hair was beginning to grow back where it had been shaved. Two weeks after that, and she was back to her old self. I have relived that day many, many times and have offered prayers of thanksgiving to the Good Lord for sparing the life of my little fuzzy-faced Wire.

7

More Fur Than Feathers

When Josie was three years old, I was invited to return to North Dakota for an October pheasant hunt. This would be my first time back to the farm where my Brittany, Patches, had been shot and killed four years earlier. My son, Jesse, would join Josie and me for this adventure.

My friend, Randy, whose dad still owned the 2000-acre farm, would be making the fourteen-hour drive with his daughter, Betsy, and two sons, Brett and Eli. They would be staying for a week, and we only had a long weekend, so it was decided that Jesse and I would drive my truck, and Randy and his kids would drive their van.

Many thoughts of my last trip to North Dakota swirled through my mind as we drove west on Interstate 94 through Minnesota and into the Dakotas. That was when my dog Patches was killed. I could still recall the sound of that first gunshot, then the horrible howling which fell silent at the second shot that ended the life of my little dog. The events replayed in my mind as vividly as if it had happened only four days earlier instead of four years, the agonizing hours that followed trying to find Patches, being lied to by the man who had shot him; Randy coming back to the truck carrying a black plastic bag that held the lifeless body of my dog and handing me the collar with Patches' identification tags jangling as they had when he ran through the fields. Finally, waiting by the truck while Randy and his brothers dug the grave where we buried Patches on a high butte overlooking the farm, and stacking rocks on top of the loose ground to prevent scavenging coyotes from getting at Patches.

So, it was with mixed emotions that we arrived at Randy's parents' home in Bismarck where we would stay for the long weekend hunt. We enjoyed a wonderful dinner with pleasant conversation and then called it a day. I took Josie for one last walk around the yard then bedded her down in her crate in the garage. I held her fuzzy face in my hands and looked into her brown eyes as her bobbed tail wagged expectantly, beating out a rapid pattern on the side of the crate. I promised her that the same fate would not befall her on her first North Dakota pheasant hunt as had Patches. I kissed her wet nose, closed and secured the crate door, and headed off to bed. Sleep came reluctantly as it always does on the eve of a special hunt, but, eventually, I was able to drift off.

We were up and at 'em at the crack of dawn. Randy's mom had prepared a wonderful breakfast to send us on our way - pancakes, eggs, ham, hash browns, juice and coffee. With full bellies and high hopes for a great day afield, we loaded up the vehicles for the one-hour drive to the farmstead.

As we pulled off the highway and onto the gravel road that leads to the farm, Josie began to whimper and whine with excitement. She has always had an uncanny knack of knowing when the start of a hunt was close at hand. Maybe she can detect the excitement that I feel, but I don't think that I actually whimper with excitement!

Josie could hardly contain herself as I opened the tailgate and released the catch on the door to her crate. I slipped the Swiss bell around her neck and tightened the collar that would indicate to me where she was at all times - especially in the tall grass where I could not see her. I am not a fan of beeper collars which emit a high-pitched sound at regular intervals while the dog is moving and another sound when the dog goes on point. I'm old school in many things, and a tinkling bell is music to my ears!

In no time at all, we had our boots laced, our blaze-orange hats were in place, and our guns loaded. Game on! Off we went! Josie quartered beautifully in front of the line of hunters. As the name of her breed suggests - German Wirehaired Pointer - when Josie catches the scent of a game bird in the field in front of her, she "freezes" with her nose pointing to the location on the ground where the bird is hiding. She has been trained to stay "on point" until I move ahead of her and flush the bird into the air or the bird takes off running which is a whole other type of adventure!

We were only out for about ten minutes when the tinkling of the Swiss bell fell silent signaling that Josie was on point. I hurried ahead to where the bell was last heard. There she stood not moving a muscle - only her nostrils flaring with each breath. She was locked in a classic pose with her left front paw off the ground. She was staring intently at a clump of brush about ten feet off the tip of her nose. I called Betsy and Brett over to position them for the best shot when the pheasant took flight. Randy reminded them that we could only shoot roosters - hens were not to be shot. Once the shooters were in place, I moved alongside Josie and softly said to her, "Whoa, girl, whoa," to keep her steady and on point. She stayed put as I moved ahead of her and began to shuffle through the brush indicated by Josie's point. To my amazement, instead of a cackling rooster breaking the cover, a cotton tail rabbit squirted out and bolted through the tall grasses. I was so surprised that I never even raised my gun much less got off a shot.

This was the first time that Josie had ever pointed a rabbit though it would certainly not be her last! By the time our North Dakota pheasant hunt came to a close two days later, Josie would have pointed and retrieved twenty roosters. She also pointed a couple of dozen rabbits, twenty-two of which we were able to put in the cooler too. Josie did not, however, retrieve a single rabbit. That was just not in her nature. But her ability to find and point bunnies made for a most memorable hunt that yielded more fur than feathers.

A couple of weeks after the trip to North Dakota, we had Randy and Pam and their kids over for a rabbit and pheasant dinner to celebrate Betsy's first-ever cottontail kill. A wonderful time was had by all. Josie continues to point cottontail rabbits back home in Wisconsin more than ten years after her first bunny point in North Dakota.

8

Folly in the Field

GETTING UP A half hour after the alarm first went off, I realized that we would never get to the farm in time for the morning flight of Canada geese. I roused my two sons from their beds. Ben was a junior in high school, and Jesse was in seventh grade. In a hushed voice, so as not to wake their mother, I explained to them that we were really late in getting up, and that they had to hurry. Jesse was at a bit of a disadvantage, however, because he had recently suffered a broken ankle and was sporting a plaster cast from his toes up to his knee. Nevertheless, he was eager to get out for the goose hunt - crutches and all.

The sun was climbing into the Eastern sky as we pulled into the farmyard an hour later. Another truck was already parked next to the barn, so I knew that we would not have the fields to ourselves this morning. "Serves me right for oversleeping," I scolded myself as we piled out of the truck. Josie was already whining excitedly, anticipating a new adventure.

We unloaded the bags of field decoys, shotguns and let Josie out of her crate for the ten-minute trek to the area near the creek where we planned to hunt. My fears of somebody else already set up in the tall weeds were realized when we spied the spread of decoys that had been set up alongside of the bulrushes. Ben and I were each carrying a bag of decoys, and I carried Jesse's shotgun along with mine. Jesse was hobbling along the path on his crutches. We stopped about a hundred yards from the creek to devise a Plan B since we would not be hunting in the cover of the bulrushes and cattails.

The decision was made to cross the creek and set up the decoys along a fence row overlooking a small field near the cow pasture. We walked down to the edge of the creek. Jesse waited on the bank while Ben and I waded across. There was only about a foot of water in the creek, but the footing was difficult, the bottom strewn with rocks and clumps of earth with weeds growing from them. Ben and I made our way across the forty feet of water and muck and set down the bags of decoys. Josie was thoroughly enjoying her romp in the muddy water. Ben stayed with the decoys while I crossed back over to get Jesse. He got up on my back (pony-back-ride style) and held his crutches in front of me as I started back across once more, my arms locked under his legs to keep him firmly in place. The going was slow as I could not see the clumps of earth and bowling-ball-sized rocks hiding beneath the surface of the standing water. All was fine until we were about six steps from the other side. That is when I stumbled on a submerged rock and lost my balance. "Hang on, Jesse!" I yelled as I struggled to regain my balance. Sadly, it was not to be, and I fell backwards, pinning Jesse beneath me. I struggled to my feet and spun around to see how Jesse was doing. I gasped in disbelief as I watched air bubbles escaping from his now submerged cast as the icy water filled his cast while he lay on his back in the creek. I leaned down and scooped Jesse up in my arms, dirty creek water trickling out the bottom of his cast over his bare toes. He was soaked to the bone and already shivering.

I carried Jesse the last few steps to dry ground and set him down and helped him out of his hunting coat and the several soggy shirts he was wearing. I took off my jacket and wrapped him up in it. The three of us huddled together and talked about what to do next. I suggested we cancel the hunt and head back home. Jesse, however, would not hear of it. He really wanted to stay and hunt. So I got him situated on my back once again and carried him the last hundred yards to the fence row. Ben carried one of the bags of decoys and started to set them out while I walked back to get the other bag of Canada geese decoys, Jesse's wet clothes, and our guns. Josie, of course, came with me as her bobbed tail wagged happily as she scampered along and sloshed in the creek.

I made the return trip back to where the boys were hunkered down among the rocks and tall grass of the fence row, put out the other dozen and a half decoys and settled in next to Jesse. He was very cold and shivering noticeably. I tore open several portable hand warmers, shook them to activate the chemicals and began stuffing them into Jesse's cast. I don't know if the hand warmers that I stuffed into his cast did much to warm him up, but at least the shivering lessened.

Twenty minutes after we were all set up, a pair of honkers materialized above a corn field north of our position. "A pair at three o'clock,"

I whispered, and we all settled a little lower in our cover. I reached over and grabbed Josie's collar with my right hand and pulled her tight up against me. "Easy girl," I whispered as her eyes scanned the sky, as if she knew exactly what was developing. With my left hand, I found the goose call hanging on a lanyard around my neck. I blew a couple of long, loud hail calls. Josie began to squirm, and I tightened my grip on her collar. "Easy, girl." Another blast on the call. "They're turning!" A couple of short honks - a little softer this time. They kept coming. A hundred and fifty yards. One hundred. Seventy-five. They were coming right into the decoys. At about fifty yards, however, they spooked and flared. It was now or never. "Take 'em!" I yelled. Ben and I jumped to our feet and unloaded on the geese. Jesse, unable to stand, stayed sitting and fired from that position.

One of the geese tumbled from the sky, but the other escaped unharmed. Josie, having watched the big Canada fold and fall, marked the spot where the bird came down. A moment later she was back, the goose held firmly in her mouth. High fives all around. Jesse was again shivering uncontrollably. We decided to call it a day. We gathered up the decoys. Jesse was able to walk on his crutches, though the going was slow moving through the pasture towards the truck. Walking on his own, however, slowed the progress but helped him warm up.

Needless to say, my wife was not at all happy with the outcome of our little hunting adventure. We had to take Jesse in to to have the cast cut off and replaced. Ironically, when the cast had been cut off, the new x-rays indicated that his ankle had sufficiently healed that a new cast was not necessary. I tried to explain to my wife that it all actually turned out for the best, and that dropping Jesse in the creek was a good thing, but she was not buying it!

9

Don't Drink the Water

A friend of a friend knew a guy who knew a guy who had a place in Iowa where we could stay when we headed over for a weekend of chasing pheasants. He and a buddy purchased the house for the sole purpose of having a place to hunt pheasants in Iowa. So for the majority of the year, nobody lived in the house. All we would have to do is adjust the setting on the thermostat, and we would be in business.

Jesse and I loaded up the truck on a cold Thursday evening so we could head out right after school the next day. On Friday afternoon once I got home from work and Jesse got home from school, we loaded Josie into the back seat of the truck, punched the coordinates into the GPS and headed west. Our destination was a dot on the map - a little town with less than two hundred people.

In November, the sun sets before five o'clock, so it was pretty dark by the time we crossed over the Mississippi River into the land of the Hawkeyes. Jesse was driving when we arrived in the little town where the house in which we were to stay was located. The last line of the directions read: "The house is across the road from the church just before the road turns to gravel." Well, it was about ten o'clock at night when we arrived. Very few of the houses in town had any lights on at this time of the night, and unfortunately for us, there were two houses across the road from the church. Josie stirred on the back seat and began to whimper with anticipation as Jesse pulled to a stop between the two houses. Both were pitch dark - one of which was the house in which we were to spend the night. But which one? We reread the directions. We looked at the church across the street and then at the two houses.

We decided to try the one on the right. I left Josie in the truck where she whined and cried as I exited the truck to check out the situation. The steps leading to the front porch creaked as I ascended them. Visions of an axe murderer leaping out of the shadows flashed through my mind as I formed a fist and knocked on the door in the darkness. Nothing. I waited a minute and knocked again. Nothing. Now I was faced with another decision; do I turn the door knob, and if the door is not locked, do I walk into the house? The alternative of sleeping in the truck all night and waiting until morning when the residents of the house might be up and about did not appeal to me. Delaying the inevitable for another moment, I knocked a third time. No lights. No sounds from within. I took hold of the door knob and slowly turned it. I could feel the mechanism in the door knob release, and the door creaked open a few inches - then a foot. A wave of stale, moldy-smelling air emanating confirmed that I had the right house. I pushed the door open all the way and stepped across the threshold and into the front room. I felt along the wall until my fingers found a light switch. Light flooded the room, and I squinted against the sudden brightness. As my eyes became accustomed to the light, I looked around the bare room noting only a folding chair and a bare mattress on the floor. I was pretty sure that I had the right house, but the thought lingered in my mind that perhaps the owner of house was actually upstairs, even now, loading a gun and would be tip toeing down the stairs to deal with these late-night intruders!

I returned to the truck and let Josie out. Jesse and I made several trips and soon had the truck emptied. We set about exploring the house. In a word, it was filthy. The refrigerator contained spoiled, moldy food. The bathroom was really awful; the tub and sink appeared not to have been cleaned in months.

It was about fifty degrees in the house so a search for the thermostat was the next order of business. Once we found it, we programmed the furnace to bring the temp up to seventy. The clanging and banging coming from the basement as the furnace kicked in was pretty unsettling as was the distinct odor of heating oil. We wondered if the whole place was gonna go up in flames - and if anybody in the neighborhood would mind! Jesse and I decided we would leave our food in the cooler, and we rolled out sleeping bags on two of the bare mattresses lying on the livingroom floor and decided to turn in. Before doing so, I took Josie out for one last potty break, then gave her a drink of water, and we settled in for the night.

The clanging of the furnace and the offensive air made for a fitful night's sleep for us. In the morning, we had a bagel and jug of OJ from the cooler then headed out to find a friendly farmer willing to let us hunt on his property. After getting turned down by the first two, the third farmer was willing to let us hunt his property. It was a large grassy stretch that bordered a cut corn field. I slipped the Swiss bell around Josie's neck, eased a couple of shells into my side-by-side, and we were off. We had not gone a hundred yards into the field when Josie bumped a rooster who did not want to sit tight for us. It was a long way out, but Jesse and I both let it fly with a couple of shots. The big ring-neck seemed to flinch but did not fall. That bird would prove to be the only shooting we would have that day. Indeed, for the whole trip!

We hunted that particular property for a couple of hours without putting up another rooster. We spent the rest of the day driving around from farm to farm asking permission to hunt fields and hedgerows. Mostly, the landowners were agreeable to having us hunt their property. Unfortunately, we did not see another rooster.

As the sun began to dip lower in the western sky, we decided to call it a day and headed for a nearby town for a bite to eat. We found a little restaurant and gobbled down a burger then drove back to the run-down house where we would spend the night. I parked the truck in front of the house, let Josie out for a quick potty break, then we climbed the steps to the porch. As the door swung open, we were again greeted with the foul aroma of stale, moldy air. The prospect of spending another night in the dirty surroundings was not particularly appealing, but we were there, and we were tired from a long day afield. We were also a little disappointed by the fact that while we had a wonderful time, we did not have any birds to show for our efforts.

We crawled into our sleeping bags for another try at a good night's sleep. I was awakened about dawn by the sound of Josie's whimpering. I came awake suddenly, remembering where I was at the first smell of the musty air in the house. It was very strange behavior for Josie, who had worked hard for hours the day before and should have been fast asleep for several more hours. But the whimpering continued as Josie moved over to stand by the door. Obviously, she wanted to go out. I opened the door and stepped onto the porch as Josie scampered down the steps and onto the scraggly grass. In just a few seconds, I realized what was going on as she had a terrible bout of diarrhea. Josie walked around in a couple of small circles then began to heave and throw up. She was in pretty rough shape. I remembered at that moment that I had given her water from the faucet in the house when we got back to town after the hunt. I would never have drunk water from the house, but Josie drinks from puddles and streams all of the time while we are hunting. Whatever was in the house water was apparently much worse than what is found out in the fields. Josie squatted again and repeated the whole process a second time. The expression "Sick as a Dog" came to mind. After a few more minutes, I decided it was safe to bring her back into the house.

Jesse was waking up and complained of having a stomach ache, feelings of nausea, and a headache. He did not feel like eating let alone hunting but said that Josie and I should go out again as long as we had driven all this way to hunt. I asked him about drinking water, but he assured me he had not even touched a faucet in the house. Bottled water only. Jesse suffers from allergies, and I shuddered to guess what was floating around in the air in the house.

It only took us fifteen minutes to pack up, throw our gear and guns in the truck, turn the thermostat back down and start our return trip home. Josie was curled up in the back seat. Jesse reclined his seat back as far as it could go and tried to get some sleep. We stopped at almost every wayside on the way home with both of my travelling companions needing frequent breaks!

I pulled into our driveway six hours later thankful for my wife, Cindy, and how clean she keeps our little home. I made sure to tell her so as soon as we got inside.

10

Flooded Timber

After reading articles about duck hunting in flooded timber for many years, I decided to arrange such a trip. On the internet, I found a guide in Arkansas who hunted primarily flooded rice fields. My son, Jesse, and I would be driving down over Christmas vacation for two days of chasing waterfowl.

It was with much anticipation and excitement that we loaded all of our gear and our beloved Josie into the truck and headed south. One of the most interesting events of the drive to Arkansas occurred in Missouri when we stopped to eat at the Home of the Throwed Rolls Restaurant. We were seated at long tables with other diners when a voice called out from across the room, "Who wants a roll?" Hands shot up all across the restaurant. The young man pushing a cart of freshly baked rolls began to throw the rolls to customers! He threw with amazing accuracy. Most of the guests were able to catch the rolls that sailed toward them. It was great fun, and Jesse and I talked about that meal for years afterward.

The drive down took about thirteen hours, and it was well past sundown by the time we arrived at the bunkhouse where we would be staying; it was pitch dark and well after suppertime. Our guide, Jim, was there along with his wife, his mother and two kids. A couple of dogs were there as well. We sat down to a wonderful spaghetti dinner and talked about the next morning's hunt. Jesse and I learned that a sudden cold snap had frozen all of the flooded rice fields where we were going to hunt, and that we would be travelling down to the Stuttgart area the next morning to hunt ducks in the flooded timber instead. Jim's cousin had a setup down there, and he would be taking us out into the flooded timber to hunt puddle ducks. This drive would be a hundred miles and require us to rise and shine two hours earlier than planned.

The others all left after the meal had been cleared leaving Jesse, Josie and me alone in the bunkhouse. After a last trip outside for Josie, we set the alarm for 3:30 and turned in.

Morning came early, dark and cold. We grabbed a bowl of cereal in the kitchen, fed Josie and stacked our gear by the door of the bunkhouse. Jim arrived shortly, helped us load our gear and our dog into the truck, and we were on the road to Stuttgart. Both Jesse and I dozed on the trip down. Josie was curled up on the back seat of the truck between us.

We arrived at our destination while it was still dark. The temp seemed a little warmer, but it was still pretty cold. We met Jim's cousin who led us down to the river which ran through his property. We all got settled into two jon boats for the trip out to the place where the decoys were set. Josie whimpered with anticipation as we slowly motored through the predawn darkness. I kept a firm grip on her collar as she sat on the floor of the boat in front of me to prevent her from jumping out of the boat to pursue something that she saw along the way.

The river emptied into the artificially flooded timber. A four-foot high dike had been constructed all around the perimeter of the woods and water was pumped in to flood the entire area. I could not imagine the number of gallons of water involved. After the hunting season, the water was pumped back out into the water system again which allowed the trees in the woods to stay alive and continue to grow the other ten months of the year. Without the current to keep the water from freezing in the cold temperatures, a thin crust of ice had formed on the surface as the temperature was below freezing down here, too. A crunching sound came from the bow of our boat as Jim navigated among the trees, now visible in the early morning light. We arrived at the opening where we would hunt, a couple dozen decoys locked in place by the thin skim of ice. Jim motored in between the decoys, breaking up the ice, and giving a more life-like appearance to the dekes as they now bobbed in the frigid water.

Jim showed me the platform where Josie was to sit. It was strapped to an oak tree and was positioned about four inches above the water which was about up to my waist as I slowly walked in my waders; I was still amazed by the feat of the flooded timber. Jesse was situated on the other side of the decoy spread, blending into the shadow of a tree trunk, about thirty yards from where I leaned against the tree next to Josie who was looking stylish in her camo-colored neoprene vest! The vest would not only help her stay warm but would also help with buoyancy if she had to swim a long ways after a downed duck. The only open water was in the area where the decoys now bobbed and the places where the hunters or boats had recently been. Otherwise, there was maybe a quarter-inch layer of ice on the water.

As I looked through the tree tops that formed the canopy above us, I wondered how we would be able to shoot at ducks that flew overhead. I would soon find out, as I heard Jim call over from where he was hidden in some trees, a duck call in hand, "Here come three mallards from the left. Get ready." I craned my neck to try to see through the tree tops but was unable to see anything. As I heard Jesse shoot, my head jerked back around, and I realized too late that the birds were only five feet off the water - not circling overhead. He knocked a hen out of the sky, and the bird hit the ice and skimmed along without breaking through. The duck had a broken wing but was in the process of waddling its way to safety. At the shot, Josie leapt off her platform into the water, swimming towards the injured fowl. The most serious problem was that Josie was unable to climb up onto the ice where she would have run down the duck in a matter of seconds, but she kept breaking through the thin crust of ice as she paddled frantically after the mallard. I gave chase, as much as somebody walking in waders in four feet of water can do! I followed the open channel that Josie created as she pursued our quarry. I could not get a shot at the duck because Josie was right between the duck and me.

The duck was getting away as it was pretty slow going for Josie to break up the ice and keep moving when she could not touch the ground. When the duck got thirty-five yards ahead of Josie, and it seemed like she would make good her escape, she made a fatal mistake and veered off to the right. That gave me a clear shot as Josie was now out of the line of vision. I quickly shouldered my Remington and fired. The duck did a somersault and lay still on the ice. A few minutes later Josie had the duck in her mouth and was on her way back. I hollered words of encouragement as my dog completed one of the most memorable retrieves of her life.

Once I had the duck in hand and got Josie back onto the safety of her platform, I could see that both of her front feet were badly cut and bleeding from breaking through the ice. She had torn two toe nails all the way down to the pads, and she was breathing heavily from the exertion of the retrieve, but the look in her big brown eyes and the thumping of her little stub of a tail said, “This is the best hunting trip ever!”

We collected six ducks that day, though none of the retrieves was as dramatic as the first one. At the end of shooting time, we climbed back into the jon boats and threaded our way among the trees on our way to the boat landing. I thanked God for the opportunity to experience this day with Jesse and Josie and for bringing us all safely back from our first-ever flooded timber duck hunt.

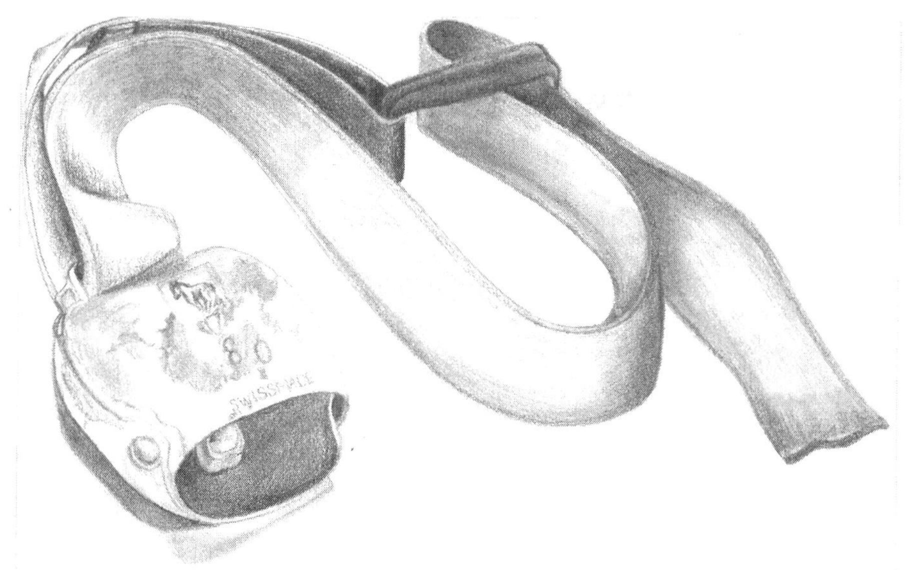

11

Locked Out

What could be more fun than a pheasant hunt in South Dakota? The youth pastor at our church had grown up on farm in South Dakota, and I made arrangements to meet up with his dad who would show me some places where we could hunt out there.

My son, Jesse, who was fifteen years old, was thrilled to make the trip. Teachers Convention meant the last Thursday and Friday of October were "no school" days so we would have a four-day weekend for our hunting adventure. We loaded Josie and our gear into my Toyota pickup truck on Wednesday evening and headed west for the seven-hundred-mile trek to the little town of Murdo which is little more than a speck on the map. Since Jesse did not have a driver's license, I would be doing all of the driving.

I didn't start getting drowsy until we were in Minnesota - five hours into the journey. Anticipating the need to stop for a snooze along the way, we had thrown a couple of sleeping bags in the truck. The mercury was hovering around 20 degrees as we pulled into a rest stop along I-94. I put Josie on a leash and took her out for a quick and chilly walk. I settled her back into the jump seat, gave her a snack, then settled into my sleeping bag to catch a cat nap and recharge my batteries. Jesse had already gotten himself snuggled into his bag after reclining his seat. Josie whimpered and settled in for a nap.

An hour later I awoke and was shivering in my sleeping bag. Snow was falling. Two inches had already accumulated on the hood of the truck. Squirming out of the sleeping bag, I started the truck, anxious for a little heat. The dashboard clock indicated it was 2:15 a.m. Josie roused in the back seat, but Jesse continued to doze, still cuddled into his sleeping bag in the passenger seat. The coffee was long gone, but I felt refreshed enough to press on, at least for a couple more hours.

The snow continued to fall and was swirling across the highway. It was a little slower going now with the truck only having two-wheel drive. The hunting gear in the back was not doing much to add weight over the back wheels.

By 4:00 a.m., I was getting pretty drowsy again, so I pulled into another rest stop, and repeated the same procedure as we had done earlier. By now, we were still on I-94 but in western Minnesota. It was still cold. It was still snowing. About 90 minutes later, I wiggled out of my sleeping bag, got back into my shoes, took Josie for another quick stroll around the parking lot, and got back on the road.

It was beginning to get light out as we crossed the South Dakota border. While the snow was beginning to taper off, it was evident that during the night it had snowed much harder in South Dakota than in Minnesota with six or seven inches of accumulation on the ground. The remainder of the trip was uneventful, and we arrived in Murdo around 9:00 a.m. Murdo is a pretty small town with only one Main Street so it was not hard to find the motel, The American Inn Express, which was an old, tired building, with seven rooms all attached side-by-side - the office being on the west end. There did not seem to be another guest in the place, as the parking lot was deserted.

We checked into our room, and I told Jesse I needed to sleep for a couple of hours, and then we would set about the business of chasing some pheasants. I crawled under the covers in one bed, while Jesse and Josie curled up on the other to watch TV while I caught some Z's.

It was not yet noon, and I was on the phone with Brian's dad letting him know that we were in town and ready to start our hunt. He apologized for the heavy blanket of snow, saying that it might significantly impact our hunting prospects and not for the better. He drove over to the motel, and we followed him in his truck a couple of miles north on snow-covered gravel roads until he pulled over and got out of his truck. We did the same. He pointed to a field next to the road which was completely covered with snow and told us this is where he had planned for us to hunt. Not a single blade of grass was showing through the snow. Clearly there were no birds lurking in the snow drifts. Our host explained that we'd hunt a neighbor's property instead which contained taller grasses and some woods which would provide some places for the birds to get out of the weather. We followed him another couple of miles and again pulled over by the side of the road.

When our host pulled over this time, we could see that there was a fairly large stand of cattails and bulrushes down along what was probably a small river in the warm weather. He instructed us on what he felt would be the best way to hunt this piece of property, wished us good luck, and headed back home. He told us to give him a call later to let him know how we did. Jesse, Josie and I spent an hour hunting the cattails and managed to bring down two of the three roosters that we put up. By now, it was late afternoon, so we headed back to town to find a restaurant to grab a bite before returning to the motel for some much needed shut eye.

The decision was made to not set an alarm - just to get up when we woke up the next morning. We awoke about 8:30 a.m. and talked about where to hunt that day. A continental breakfast was part of the deal, so Jesse and I left Josie in the room while we walked down to the office for the continental breakfast which consisted of hot chocolate/coffee and a donut. I could see Josie through the window as we headed to the office. She was anxious about being left alone and was up on her hind feet with her front paws on the door. When Jesse and I returned to the room a few minutes later with breakfast in hand - including a donut for Josie - we were surprised to discover that the door was locked! We had not locked the door and had not even taken the room key with us, Murdo being such a small, safe, and crime-free community and our room being the only one with guests. Through the window, I could see our key lying on the table next to the bed. Somehow, Josie had managed to set the door lock from the inside when she was pawing at the door in an attempt to get out when Jesse and I left her alone not three minutes earlier!

I went back to the office and explained our predicament to the woman on duty assuming she would pull a master key out of the drawer and open our door for us. Wrong. Instead she handed me a cardboard box that contained no less than 80 assorted and miscellaneous keys, none of them labeled or tagged. She explained that there was, in fact, no such thing as a master key, since the locks on the doors had been randomly replaced several times over the many decades that the motel had been in existence. There may or may not be a key in that box that would open the door. Twenty minutes later, I had tried every single key, but to no avail. Back to the office with the bad news. The manager informed me that her husband was down at the diner having breakfast with friends, but that she would call him there and explain our situation, and maybe he had a key.

While Jesse and I stood outside our room and ate our donuts and sipped our cold beverages, Josie had worked herself into a bit of a lather wanting only to be reunited with us. So near and yet so far! Reassuring her through the window that she was all right did little to lower her anxiety level, as she whimpered and paced and scratched and sniffed at the inside of the door.

Finally, a truck pulled into the parking lot and stopped in front of our room. A man got out of the truck holding a huge ring of keys. He introduced himself to us as the owner of the motel. The tenth or eleventh key slid into the lock, tripped the tumblers, and the door swung open. Josie bounded into my arms - thrilled to be back with us again.

The next two days provided lasting memories - getting stuck in a snowbank and having to walk up to a neighboring farm to have him pull us out with his tractor, hearing stories of our youth pastor's growing up from his parents, the time spent with my son, and yes, shooting a bunch of birds!

12

Mud Hen Stew

Plans were made for a duck hunting trip out to Iowa with both of my boys - Ben and Jesse - and, of course, Josie. A friend and I had gone out there the year before to hunt snow geese on a guided hunt. The hunt turned out to be a bust with only one bird even shot at - and missed - by eight hunters in layout blinds over a two-day hunt. The guide, perhaps experiencing a little sympathy for our bad luck, offered to guide us on a fall goose hunt.

Thus it was, that Ben, Jesse, Josie and I found ourselves in northern Iowa with the Sure Shot Guide Service. Our one-day Canada goose hunt yielded only one honker, not much of an improvement over the previous spring, but we did have two more days to hunt ducks while we were out there. Our guide had given us a map with several area lakes circled. Wishing us better luck with ducks than we had with the geese, the guide left us to our own devices.

The three of us studied the map after supper that evening and decided on one of the lakes as our early morning destination for the next day. The following morning found us at the boat launch shortly after sunrise. The day was overcast, the temperature was in the forties and the wind was howling out of the west at over thirty miles an hour! This wind raised some anxiety as the waves would be significant once we were out in open water. We had to motor down a long, cattail-lined channel to get to the open water, and I saw that we had six or seven inches of clearance between the water and the gunwale. Not a large margin of safety with three guys, all their gear, a dog and a couple of bags of decoys.

We continued to putt along through the channel at about three miles an hour - the open water now visible at the end of the channel. A moment later, we had cleared the channel and were in open water. We had not gone twenty feet when the waves began breaking over the bow of the boat, each one pouring several gallons of water into the boat. At this rate, we would be swamped within two minutes! I could see the look of panic on the boys' faces. We were in serious trouble. I spun the boat around and pointed the bow back to the safety of the channel, but now we were caught in the grip of the wind, and we were taking on water at an alarming rate as the waves were now breaking over the stern. I yelled for the boys to start bailing with whatever they could find, as the boat settled ever lower in the water. We were inching our way back to the channel, fighting against the wind and waves. All of the water in the bottom of the boat made it very sluggish to handle, but I was able to keep the nose pointed in the right direction.

The wind had crumpled the thin-wall conduit that served as the frame for hanging the sheets of camouflage twisting it into pretzel-shaped forms. The piles of camouflage now littering the floor made it more difficult for Ben and Jesse to bail the water out of the boat as I struggled to get us back into the protection of the channel. Ben grabbed the coffee can filled with with miscellaneous supplies and dumped them out and was bailing furiously. Jesse was splashing the water back out over the gunwale using the cover of one of our five-gallon buckets. Josie's fuzzy face was sticking out from the heap of camo, her big brown eyes wide, her fur thoroughly soaked.

We finally made it back into the channel out of the grip of the wind and away from the waves that had threatened to swamp us. I shut off the motor. The boys slumped down on their seats. Josie crawled out from under the debris of the blind. Ben, Jesse and I looked at each other for a brief moment without saying a word, considering what a close call we just had. Then we all broke into hysterical laughter and began re-telling the harrowing experience we just shared.

Ten minutes later, we had most of the water out of the boat which was still nestled safely within the confines of the channel. I fired up the outboard, and we continued motoring back towards the boat launch from which we left only a half hour earlier. I had not noticed another channel branching off the main channel on our way out to the lake, but I swung our little boat into this little waterway bypass. Fifteen seconds later, it opened into a small, protected pond, maybe thirty yards across. A flock of mud hens that had been lazily lounging along the edge of the pond was alarmed by our sudden appearance. They all began running across the water, flapping their wings as the their legs propelled them toward safety, eventually becoming airborne.

I have never been a fan of eating mud hens, but I told the boys about my Uncle Bud, my dad's brother, who was quite a waterfowler when he was still alive and the holder of numerous state skeet shooting championships. He used to shoot mud hens while duck hunting, saving them up in his freezer for his annual mud hen stew, which was a tradition enjoyed by my uncle and his hunting buddies at the close of every duck hunting season.

We quickly decided that this would be a great opportunity to start such a tradition of our own, especially since the mud hens were tucked back in the criss cross of channels and ponds, away from the pounding waves on the big lake. For the next hour we putted and poled and poked around, shooting at the pointy-billed waterfowl as they raced back and forth along the surface of the water or flew helter skelter just a foot or two above the cattails and reeds that formed the ponds and channels. At times, it was like a shooting gallery with all three of us blasting away with reckless abandon! There were twenty-three mud hens laying in the bottom of the boat when we did get back to the boat launch.

We never had so much shooting in such a short time, and even though they were only mud hens, it was quite a day to remember, especially since it appeared initially that there would be no shooting this morning at all.

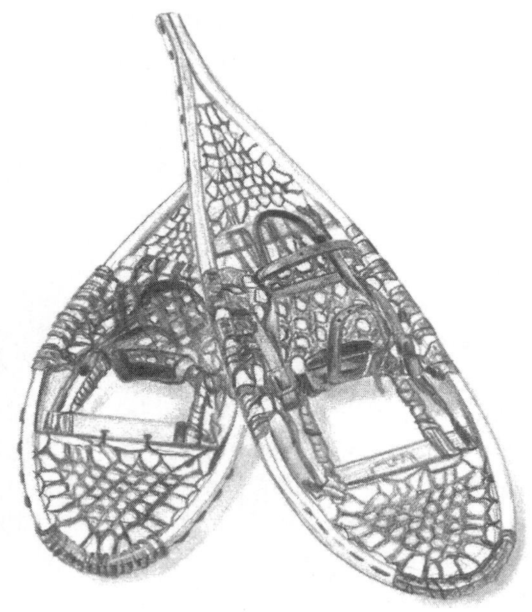

13

Pastor's First Hunt

THE IDEA OF taking our pastor on a pheasant hunt came to me one Sunday morning after church while talking with a long-time friend, hunting companion and one of the most serious hunters I know. Kenny and I were chatting about making plans to go out to South Dakota for a muzzle-loader hunt when our senior pastor strolled over to join in the conversation. Jason commented that he had done a little turkey and deer hunting but had never actually killed any wild game.

Kenny and I quickly hatched a plan to take the pastor out for a pheasant hunt. I contacted a game farm in the sleepy little town of Theresa, in Dodge County, to set it up for the following weekend.

On the drive up to the farm, Kenny and I explained some of the basics of a game farm pheasant hunt to Pastor Jason - planted birds, yes, but almost a guarantee of shooting. We talked about hunting with a pointing dog, as Josie was along, and she was charged with the responsibility of finding the birds for us. We talked about hens and roosters, both of which would be fair game on this outing.

The sun was shining brightly in a cloudless blue sky as we pulled into the driveway leading to the farm. The mercury hovered around 30 degrees. About 16 inches of snow blanketed the ground. A beautiful day for the pastor's first pheasant hunt. A few minutes later, the three of us were sitting at the kitchen table of the farmhouse having a cup of coffee and signing the liability forms with the proprietor's wife while the owner headed out on his four-wheeler to release our birds.

Twenty minutes later, it was show time! We walked back out to the truck to lock and load. Jason would use my Wingmaster pump, and I would be carrying my side by side. I showed him how the shells were inserted and ejected and how the safety operated. I handed him one of my spare blaze-orange vests - the shell holders in the two pockets already filled with number six shotshells. I donned a pair of snowshoes, but neither Jason nor Kenny wore them today. I slipped into my hunting jacket and my orange vest and slid my gun from its case.

All of this was taking much too long for Josie, and she began to whimper and whine in her crate, anxious to get on with the hunt. I opened the door of the crate and lifted her to the ground, slipped her Swiss bell around her neck, and we were off.

We worked our way across an open field and then began to follow the creek that formed the southern end of the property. Josie locked up on a patch of weeds along the edge of the creek. I could see pheasant tracks leading into the clump of cover. I called for Pastor Jason to get ready and positioned him near where Josie stood, frozen on point - the only movement was the heaving of her sides and the flaring of her nostrils with the scent of the hidden bird filling her nose. Kenny moved into a ready position 20 yards further down along the edge of the creek. I explained to Jason that I would try to get the bird to flush straight away from us out over the frozen creek where he should have a clear shot, but that sometimes the birds run instead, especially with the crust that was hard enough to support a pheasant's weight which was certainly the case today.

Once Jason was set, I moved alongside Josie, talking softly to her, "Good girl, Josie. Whoa, girl." She stood firm, eyes locked on the clump of weeds ten feet upwind. Now I could see the tail feathers of the hen huddled in the weeds. She was facing away from me towards the creek as I had hoped. Maybe this shot would go just as planned, and the bird would fly straight away, over the creek. As I took another step towards the bird, she burst from the cover, flying up and away over the creek, offering Pastor Jason a straight-away shot. "Take it, Jason!" I hollered, and his gun roared. The bird crumpled as feathers flew. Josie raced out to gather up the bird and retrieved it as Kenny and I high-fived Pastor Jason for his first-ever pheasant. I explained to Jason that since he shot it, he would have to carry it. I slipped the bird into the pouch in his vest.

Over the next hour-and-a-half, we enjoyed a wonderful hunt, shooting another five birds. On our way back to the truck, we had to cross another open area, about the size of a football field. As we neared the far edge of the field, Josie went on point again, though this time there was not a blade of grass visible above the blanket of snow covering the ground. I called over to Kenny and Jason, and they joined me where

Josie stood, again rock solid, her fuzzy face pointing towards an indentation in the snow. We fanned out to cover any possible escape route. With my snowshoes on, I could not use my foot to excavate down to where maybe a bird was burrowed under the snow. We were only 20 feet from the edge of the woods, and I wondered why a bird would choose to hide out in an open field when the relative safety of the woods was so near. I knelt down so I could use my gloved hand to dig down into the snow. Josie, standing right next to me, kept her eyes riveted on the same place. I had only dug out a few handfuls of snow when the hen burst from a snowy den, but instead of taking to the air, she made a run for it - literally! It couldn't - or wouldn't - fly, but boy could she run...straight for the woods. "Don't shoot! Don't shoot!" I yelled, fearing that Josie might get hit, as she was already in hot pursuit. Josie chased the bird into the woods where the pheasant attempted to find refuge in a small pile of brush but came squirting out the other end as Josie began to dig her way into the pile.

Kenny, Jason and I started towards the woods to see how the drama would unfold. We were quite surprised when the pheasant - with Josie still on her tail - came streaking along the crusted snow directly towards us, as we were still in the open field. The crazy bird, clearly unable to fly, was going to run right through the middle of the three of us. As she neared, I raised my snowshoed right foot as high as I could, and as the bird ran past, I slammed the shoe down, pinning the bird to the ground in the webbing. What a surprising turn of events!

Jason watched in disbelief as I reached under the snowshoe, plucked out the bird, and quickly dispatched it. "You killed that bird with your bare hand," was all he said. Twenty minutes later, we were on our way home.

The next weekend, we all gathered at our home for a wild game feast. Pastor Jason brought two different, and delicious, pheasant dishes!

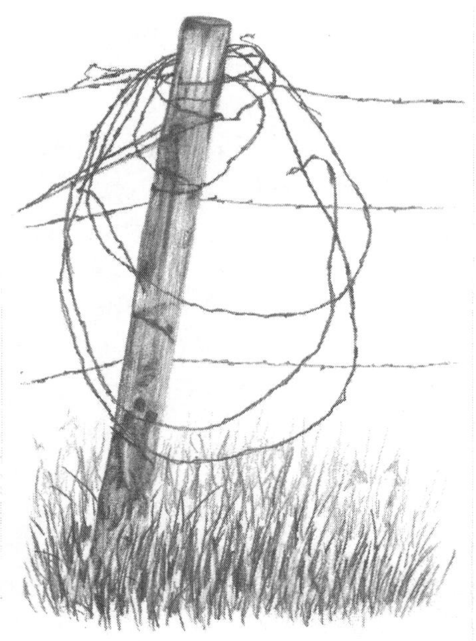

14

Nicked Ear

Josie and I were on a pheasant hunt at the Ozaukee County Fish and Game Club. It was January, and there was a beautiful blanket of deep snow covering the ground. I decided to hunt the section of the property nearest the club house. Because it was nearby, I decided that we would walk from the parking lot through the trap fields and enter the hunting field on foot. It was one of those rare weekends when few guys came out to hunt, and Josie and I had our designated area all to ourselves.

We entered the field and had been hunting for about a half hour when I noticed drops of blood on the snow. I was puzzled by the fact that there were no pheasant tracks in the snow near the crimson specks, so I called Josie over and noticed that she had nicked her left ear, perhaps on a thorn or on a barbed-wire fence. The cut was on the very edge of her ear where the skin was paper thin. There is, however, a small vein that runs along the entire perimeter of the ear, and she clearly had cut that vein. I could see that a band aid would do nothing to stop the bleeding, so I scooped up a handful of snow and pressed it onto the cut, holding Josie's head still with my other hand by pulling her tightly against me. After five minutes, I checked again. The drip, drip, drip continued unabated. I decided to call it a day, and Josie and I headed back to the truck in the parking lot.

If anything, the bleeding had increased slightly during the trek back. I got the first-aid kit out of the truck and removed the roll of gauze. After fashioning a 4 x 4 gauze square, I pressed it onto Josie's ear and applied pressure to stop the bleeding. I told Josie that she would be okay as she looked up at me with those big brown eyes. Her stubby little tail never stopped wagging. Five minutes of pressing the compress onto the wound did little to stem the flow of blood. Another ten minutes of continuing to apply pressure to the cut yielded the same result. Now I was becoming a little worried. I lifted Josie into the crate in the back of the truck and began the thirty-mile drive back home. En route, I called my vet and was told to bring her right in.

I arrived at the Family Pet Clinic forty minutes later and was shocked to see the amount of blood that was in the bottom of her crate. We received preferential treatment and were ushered right into an exam room. I was given another wad of gauze to hold on her ear while I waited. By now, Josie's whole left side was covered with blood all stemming from the tiny cut on the edge of her ear. The veterinarian arrived shortly and, upon examination, confirmed that the little vein that runs along the perimeter of her ear had been severed. The problem was that because her ear was so thin at that point, stitches or staples were not an option. The best approach was to wrap the ear in gauze, first of all, and then wind the bandages around her whole head to hold the gauze in place. Ten minutes later, all that could be seen on Josie's fuzzy little face were her eyes, nose and mouth. She looked like a mummy with yards of bandages wrapped around her head!

I put the leash back on Josie and led her out of the clinic and back to the truck, opting to put her in the front seat with me in lieu of back in the crate now red with her blood. She did not seem to be in any pain in spite of how pitiful she looked. She sat on the seat and looked out the window, just like always.

Josie had not eaten all day, so I brought her into the basement where her food and water dishes were kept. She trotted over to her bowl of kibble and began to eat hungrily. Satisfied that she would be alright, I headed back upstairs.

An hour later, Josie appeared in the kitchen...minus her head dressing! The bleeding had begun again, and she was dripping blood all over the kitchen floor. Her coat now more red than brown and grey. I grabbed the roll of gauze, re-wrapped her ear, then rewound several yards of bandaging around her head. After cleaning up the floor, I descended the steps back into the basement. Several of the carpeted steps showed red spots. At the bottom of the stairs, I stared around the room in horror. Blood was splattered everywhere - on the carpeted floor, the walls, the couch, the loveseat. It looked like somebody had been murdered! I could not believe that all of this blood came from a quarter-inch cut on the edge of Josie's ear.

I loaded Josie back into the truck and headed back to the vet's office, dialing their number on my cell phone en route. Dr. Fellenz could not believe that she had managed to get out of her bandages. He said that there was nothing to do but rewrap her, maybe just a little more tightly this time. Fifteen minutes later we were back on our way home to deal with that mess.

My wife, Cindy, and I did not even attempt to clean up the blood-splattered basement. We called a professional cleaning service. Even then, it took two treatments to get the blood out of the carpet, floors and furniture.

The dressing did not come off her head for three days, and by then, the bleeding had finally stopped. She has been fine ever since, but without a doubt, this has been one of the messiest misadventures we have ever had with Josie!

15

Bite of a Snickers

The neighbors across the street had a pet rabbit named Snickers which they kept in a mesh cage on the patio behind their house. Josie, being the neighborly type of dog she was, would often meander across the street to visit the neighbors, and if she could get a sniff and peak at Snickers, so much the better! Usually they would shoo her back home, or if I heard them yelling at Josie to go home, I would hustle over and retrieve her.

Oftentimes, if I were working outside or in the garage and realized Josie was no longer in our yard, I would stroll over to the neighbors' back yard and would find her standing next to Snickers' cage - looking, sniffing, and perhaps salivating ever so slightly.

One sunny summer day while I was puttering with something in the garage, however, Josie had gone AWOL, but before I discovered she had again ventured across the street to visit Snickers, I heard one of the girls screaming at the top of her lungs, "Josie, no! Stop! Josie No!" This scream was much more frantic and urgent than ever before. I jumped up and began to run down our driveway to get across the street to see what kind of mischief Josie was in, when what do I see? Snickers was racing around the corner of their house running as fast as her furry little legs could go with Josie in hot pursuit. Only a couple of steps behind Josie was one of the girls screaming hysterically for Josie to stop chasing her pet rabbit! I watched in disbelief as this comical parade headed down their driveway, across the street and into the yard of our nextdoor neighbor. In a matter of seconds I joined in, bringing up the rear of the train, also yelling at Josie to stop. Not too much chance of that happening! I am certain that there was a smirk on Josie's fuzzy face as she bore down on the pet rabbit which was running for its life.

All four of us raced around the back of our neighbor's house and then headed right for our back yard. Snickers. Josie. Kristen. PJ. Snickers dove under the wood pile in the corner of our yard. Josie was there in less than two seconds, but the rabbit was safe. Kristen was crying when she and I got to Josie. I grabbed her collar and took her to her kennel while Kristen tried to coax Snickers out from under the wood pile. I scolded Josie as I closed the door to the kennel. She looked at me as if to say, "I was only playing. I could have had that rabbit in the first twenty feet." She still wore that smirk, too!

I learned later that on this particular visit, Josie had actually put her front paws up on the cage, and the frightened rabbit began to run in tiny circles inside the cage which only further fueled Josie's interest. That little bit of jiggling of the cage caused the bottom to drop out depositing Snickers right at Josie's feet. And the race was on!

Ultimately, this little adventure ended well for everyone. Snickers escaped with her life. Josie had a great time playing "Chase the Bunny." Kristen got her rabbit back in one piece, not too much worse for the wear. And I got another great story for my collection of Josie's antics.

16

Whoa, Girl

My two sons and I booked a hunt at Pheasants on the Ledge, a hunt club located up in Fond du Lac County, not far from the famed Horicon Marsh. We arrived at the clubhouse about noon as we had arranged for an afternoon hunt. After lunch of a burger and fries, we got directions to our field and headed out.

It was a beautiful October day - blue sky, 50 degrees, a little wind. A perfect day to chase pheasants, and as is always the case, Josie was eager to get started. She let us know that we were taking too long to get her out of her crate by whining and whimpering. “Hang on, Josie. We’re almost ready. I know you want to get started.” I opened the door to her crate, set her on the ground, and slipped the Swiss bell around her neck.

Our field was mostly warm weather grasses, with strips of sorghum to provide cover and maybe a little variety. We walked to the edge of the field to get the wind in our face, spread out to cover about a 20-yard swath, and headed in. Josie was working really well, quartering nicely 15 or 20 yards out in front of us. Ten minutes into the hunt, a rooster flushed in between Ben and Jesse, and we had our first bird in the bag.

“Dad, Josie’s on point!” Jesse was walking along the edge of our field when he called out. Ben and I hurried over towards where he now stood. As I neared, I could see Josie was indeed on point, facing into the gentle breeze where I knew that the addictive scent of a hiding pheasant wafted towards her. I paused to consider this moment which is what Josie loved. It’s what she lived for. I wondered what was going on inside her head. Do dogs think thoughts like we do? If so, she was probably thinking, “I just love the smell of pheasants,” or “I hope these three guys don’t mess up this perfect point,” or “I can smell you, but I can’t see you. I know you’re here.”

As we got ourselves positioned for the best opportunity for a shot when the bird was flushed, I suddenly noticed a little movement in the tangle of weeds 15 feet in front of Josie’s nose. “It’s a hen,” I said to the boys in a hushed voice. “Get ready.” We were ready but not for what happened next. The bird emerged from its hiding place and began walking straight towards us. Josie stayed rock solid, her eyes locked onto the bird, now only ten feet in front of her but still closing the distance. “Whoa, girl. Easy. Whoa.” My voice was hardly more than a whisper.

Still the bird came closer now only a foot in front of Josie who still held the point. I was certain she would grab the bird in her mouth which she could now do without taking a step. "Whoa, girl." Josie stayed still while that pheasant walked right underneath her. The bird stopped, seemed to glance around, then pecked at a pebble on the ground. It was unbelievable. I had never seen anything quite like this before.

The boys and I could do nothing but stare in disbelief as this mini-drama played out in front of us. The thought crossed my mind that perhaps the bird could not fly, for whatever reason. Josie could not see the bird any longer, and she shifted around ever so slightly to keep the bird in her line of sight. That was all it took for the pheasant to prove that, yes, she could certainly fly! The hen took to the air so suddenly that all three of us were taken by surprise. It took a second or two for us to assure safe shooting lanes for everybody, flip off safeties, and shoulder our guns. By the time shots rang out, the bird was forty yards away. It was flying into the sun which further compromised our position. A few feathers flew from the bird indicating that at least some of the lead pellets had found their mark. The hen locked its wings and glided to the ground some sixty or seventy yards from where we stood still amazed by what had just happened. The bird was definitely hit but not very hard, and if it could still run, it would be quite a task for Josie to chase it down. Josie was already on the run by the time the bird landed, and we could hear the tinkling of the bell as she searched the area where the hen had come down. Yes, the bird was running, as the sound of the bell grew fainter. A few minutes later, however, the jingle jangle of Josie's bell became louder. Finally the dog came back into view with the hen, still alive, held firmly in Josie's soft mouth.

Over the years, we have had many exciting and memorable encounters with game birds but none quite as strange as the hen on the edge of the field.

17

White Hole

Morning dawned cold and breezy that Saturday in late January. The temperature registered fifteen degrees with a wind chill about zero. The sun climbed into a cloudless blue sky. Certainly a great day for a pheasant hunt; but then any day is a great day to get out and chase ring-necks!

Once the gear was loaded and Josie was safely crated in the back of the truck, we headed out on the thirty-five minute drive up to Newburg - home of the Ozaukee County Fish and Game Club. As is her style, as soon as I turned into the gravel drive leading to the club house, Josie began whimpering with excitement knowing what was to come. Protocol at the club was for every hunter to sign the logbook indicating which area he would be hunting that day. I signed up to hunt "The Cribs," so named because of the three silo-like corn cribs that were located on this particular farm. The Cribs was one of several properties leased by the hunt club for the purpose of providing pheasant hunts for the members during the hunting season. I would be hunting with Roger and his English Setters today.

At the assigned time, all of the hunters left the clubhouse and headed for their designated areas which were scattered throughout the surrounding countryside. Driving down the snow-covered road toward The Cribs, I could see that the snow was about two-feet deep which meant that the going would be pretty slow and deliberate on this wintery morning.

Josie would be sporting a brand new set of booties which my niece, Tara, had sewn for her. I first learned that Tara was in the bootie business when her Christmas letter arrived the previous December. In the letter, she chronicled her fascination with the Iditarod, the dog-sled race held in Alaska each year to commemorate the historic event in 1925, when a diphtheria epidemic threatened the lives of hundreds of people in Nome, and dog sleds were the only means available to get the serum to the sick in time. Tara had begun making booties for the mushers in the Iditarod to use on their dogs. She had agreed to sew up a set for Josie, and here we are!

Roger and I got our dogs out - Lily wearing an electronic beeper collar and Josie with her Swiss bell tinkling as she romped in the snow.

There was just a hint of a crust on the sea of white, not enough to support the weight of the dogs who were plowing through some drifts that were chest deep on them. I guessed, however, that the crust would support the weight of a running pheasant which would definitely work in favor of the birds that would, quite literally, be running for their lives if they decided to run instead of taking to the sky.

After an hour of hunting, Roger had two birds in his vest. Josie had pointed and retrieved a hen for me as well. We decided that an hour was enough for that day as both dogs and their owners were pretty well spent from the difficult walking. I chose to head back to the truck via a plowed lane which provided easy walking. Josie also came down onto the path walking along ahead of me. Her nose was constantly sniffing the air. As we neared the gravel road which would take us back to the trucks, Josie, standing in the middle of the plowed lane, went on point! There was not a blade of grass or a shrub within fifty feet of where we were - only snow. I could not imagine what was wrong with her nose that she would be on point when clearly there was no bird anywhere near. "No bird!" I called to Josie, expecting her to follow me back towards the truck. But she remained rock solid, staring intently at a set of footprints in the snow alongside the lane, probably made by a hunter from the day before, or perhaps the landowner had been out for a walk earlier in the day. I walked back to Josie and tugged slightly on her collar to get her to come with me. No luck. The strange possibility crept into my mind that a bird might be hunkered down in one of the footprints, but no pheasant tracks were to be seen anywhere.

I decided I would have to climb up into the snowbank and have a look in each of the footprints. I glanced over my shoulder and hoped that Roger was not watching as I knew I would take some good-natured ribbing from him for doing so. As I took the first step into the snow to get closer to the tracks, a hen pheasant erupted from the deep footprint not five feet from where I stood. Startled, I jumped back struggling to maintain my balance. Trying to regain my composure while watching the bird fly away, my first shot was a clean miss. The second shot found its mark, and the bird folded and tumbled back to the snow bank. Josie was already on her way to the bird by the time it dropped into the snow.

Josie retrieved the bird and then looked at me with what I am certain was a smirk, as if to imply, "No points for style on that shooting!" If dogs could chuckle, I know that she would have laughed out loud. I tucked the bird into my game pouch, scratched behind Josie's ears, and headed back to the truck.

18

Porky Problems

Josie and I were back out in North Dakota for a pheasant hunt with my good friend, Randy, to chase roosters on the same two-thousand-acre farm where he had grown up. As we began our search for the wiley ring-necked roosters through the creek bottoms, I could not help remember being out here six years earlier when my dog Patches had been shot and killed by the psycho tenant who was living in the homestead on the farm. Even after all of this time had passed, my eyes were drawn to the distant butte, where Randy and I had laid Patches to rest.

But that was then - this was now. A new day. A new dog. A new opportunity. Excitement was in the air. Josie was working very well, having pointed and put up a number of birds - some hens and some roosters. A few of the long tails actually ended up in the game bags!

We decided to take a little detour, left the creek bottoms, and headed instead up the side of a hill to see what lay beyond. Josie was wearing her Swiss bell as she always did when we were hunting in tall grass so I could keep track of her as she worked. The bell fell silent as we trudged through the waist-high grass, and I initially thought she might be locked up on another bird. I had a pretty good idea of where she was based on where I last heard the tinkling of her bell and started backtracking in that direction.

When I drew to within about ten yards of where I thought she should be, I heard her yelp and knew immediately that she was not on point. My first thought was that she had been bitten by something, and I hoped it was not a snake because I was ill-prepared to deal with a snake bite. A moment later, I came upon her in the tall grass and realized, fortunately, it was not a snake but, unfortunately, a porcupine! Josie had quills protruding from her nose as well as stuck between the toes of her front left foot.

When I glanced over at the porcupine, I could see that it had been dead for some time. Josie had not encountered a live porky at all, but the curiosity over her first encounter with any kind of a porcupine got the best of her, and she went in for a sniff and a touch. Thus began the long, painful and tedious process of extracting the porcupine quills, one at a time, using a small pair of pliers that I carried with me in my hunting vest. Porcupine quills have little barbs on them, similar to fish hooks so they do not simply poke and release. The little barbs catch on the flesh - in this case Josie's nose and in between the pads on her left foot - then the quills release from the porcupine's body and are stuck in the body of the predator.

Randy helped me hold her down while I began to remove the quills, one by one, working them as gently as I could, back and forth, back and forth, until the quills released from her - first from her nose and then from her toes. It took about a half hour, but we finally had them all out. From my first-aid pouch, I removed the tube of antibiotic ointment and smeared a little on each of her little punctures.

Josie walked a little gingerly for the next few minutes, but after that she seemed just fine. Our hunt continued successfully for the rest of the long weekend, but the lesson of the porcupine was never forgotten.

19

ACL Times Two

IN THE FALL of Josie's sixth year, just as hunting season was approaching, I noticed that she started limping a little bit, favoring her right rear leg. Then a little more of a limp... and then a little more... until she was faltering terribly. There had been times in her young life when she had had an injured paw or a cut pad or a bit of a strain after a particularly long day afield, but always she returned to normal after a few days of taking it easy. But this time she was not healing on her own. She was progressively getting worse, until she would not put any weight at all on that leg, but began to hobble around on three legs.

A trip to the vet confirmed that she actually had an ACL tear, and, as with humans, the only real fix is surgery. And, as with humans, a specialist would have to be called in to perform the operation. A canine orthopedic surgeon who specialized in repairing ACL injuries was contacted and the surgery was scheduled. During a phone conversation with the surgeon prior to the surgery, she explained that usually these ACL tears occur in older, out-of-shape dogs. Josie, however, was still a relatively young dog, was in great shape and did not have an ounce of fat on her, so it was strange that she was suffering from this ailment. The surgeon did go on to warn me that quite often, when a dog suffers an ACL tear on one side, it is very common for the animal to tear the ACL on the other side as well. Since I could not have Josie in the pain she was experiencing, there was no question but to move forward with the surgery. Well, the operation was successful, and then began the recuperation. Josie had to wear one of those funny-looking cones around her head so she could not lick or bite or otherwise get at the incision for the first few weeks. The recuperation took about five weeks and basically wiped out that hunting season.

I did have the opportunity to get up to the hunt club on several occasions and just tagged along with some of the other guys who had dogs, but it was certainly not the same as having my girl with me out in the field. But by the end of winter, Josie was back to being her old self, as good as new.

About eighteen months after the surgery, the words of the doctor came back to haunt me, as Josie began to favor her left rear leg, in much the same fashion as she done with the ACL tear on her right leg. A trip to the vet confirmed that, yes, Josie had indeed torn the ACL on her left rear leg. The X-rays also revealed that the arthritis in Josie's back and both rear legs had gotten noticeably worse in the year-and-a-half since the last surgery, and I was reminded of her brush with death when she had been hit by a car. It seemed likely that the accident had begun the onset of arthritis in my hunting partner. I had another phone conversation with the very same orthopedic specialist. Again the surgery was scheduled and again the operation was successful. And again the lengthy recuperation began. The only upside to the second ACL episode was that it occurred during the summer months and did not interfere with the hunting season.

Josie never did have any problems with her front legs, but the surgeries on both back legs were certainly something I'll never forget.

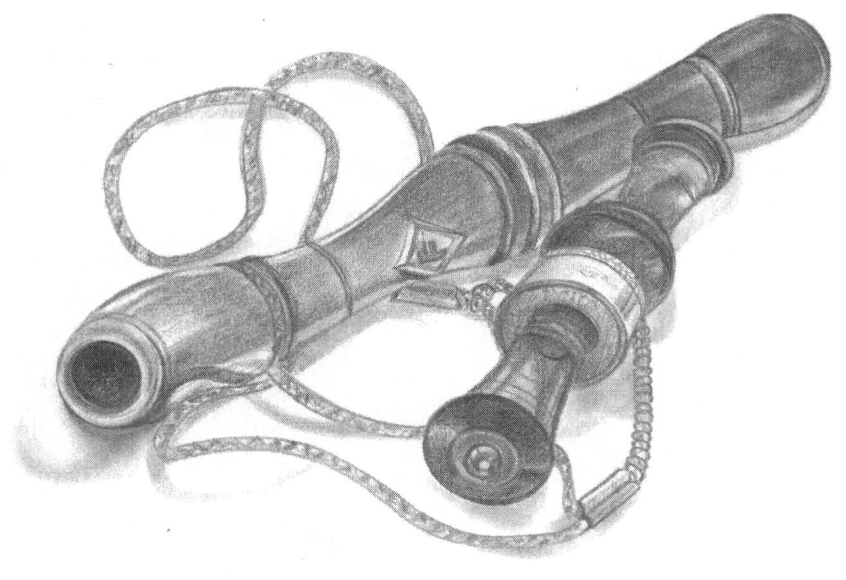

20

Calling All Geese

I received an invitation to hunt ducks with a guy I had known for several years, although we had never hunted together. We would be heading down to Lake Tichigan, which is located in Walworth County in South Central Wisconsin. Jeff is an instructor for Hunter Safety and had been hunting waterfowl for years before I met him. He has his own boat and a nice spread of decoys, but he does not have a dog. Enter Josie! One interesting point to note about Jeff is that he has been deaf since birth. He is very adept at lip reading and American sign language. I, on the other hand, cannot form but a handful of American sign language letters so I brought along a pen and pad of paper for note writing.

Jeff lived with his folks about forty minutes away from the lake. When I pulled into the driveway, I could see that Jeff already had his boat hooked up to his truck. I greeted Jeff, shook his hand, and asked him if the ducks have been flying and whether or not he was having any luck. I could see him watching my lips intently, and I found myself struggling to talk as normally as possible, but I could hear myself talking much louder than usual, as if that would make it easier for him to read my lips. He said that the duck hunting had been lukewarm this past week, but that even if the ducks are not flying, it is always great to be out in the blind. Josie and I climbed into the truck with Jeff, and we headed out.

Because Jeff had to keep his eyes on the road and could not look at me, the drive to the lake was pretty quiet. We arrived at the boat landing, and he backed the boat into the water, piled in the rest of our gear, and we were soon motoring out of the channel toward open water.

About three miles from the boat landing, Jeff had built a permanent blind along the west shore of the lake tucked in among the cattails and bulrushes on a little point which jutted out into a small, sheltered bay. It looked to be a very good spot, and it was with much anticipation that we put out a couple of dozen decoys. After hiding the boat behind the blind, we climbed into the blind and loaded our guns.

As we waited for birds to start flying, I got out my pad of paper and wrote out a question, asking him about his job and how he was able to cope with his deafness at work. I wrote several other questions - mostly making small talk. Jeff was able to answer verbally, and while his speech had that distinctive quality of the deaf population, I was able to understand what he was saying. As I was preparing to jot another question,

I glanced up and spied three mallards winging their way towards our spread flying low over the top of the cattails and pointed them out to Jeff, even as I hunkered lower into the confines of the blind. Holding my shotgun in my right hand, I reached for Josie's collar with my left, and drew her close against me to keep her from moving about and flaring the ducks. As the ducks drew nearer, I realized that usually in this situation my hunting partner and I would whisper strategies to each other. "Get ready." "Not close enough yet." "Let them circle around one more time." Then finally, "Take 'em!" I wondered how this would play out since we would not be talking to each other in hushed voices in order to coordinate our shots. This time, however, it was a moot point as the ducks altered their course taking them well out of range. I released my hold on Josie, who was now whimpering with excitement and anticipation, her stubby little tail a blur as it wagged back and forth wildly.

Since this was Jeff's gig, I decided to let him take the lead as far as when to shoot should the next flock venture closer into the air space above the blind. Even as I watched the three mallards disappear in the distance, a pair of blue-winged teal buzzed the blind coming from behind us undetected. By the time we saw them, they were already out over the decoys, and in the time it took us to shoulder our guns and click off the safeties, they were on the outside edge of our shooting range. Glancing over at Jeff, I could see that he was going to shoot, so I refocused on the two birds that were making good their escape. We each shot twice but failed to connect with our quarry. Since Josie could not see over the top of the blind, she could not see that the birds were now safely out of range. Hearing the shots signaled her to make the retrieve, and it was all I could do to call her off the retrieve as she frantically looked for a way out of the blind and into the water. "No bird! No bird!" I yelled. Finally she calmed down, and I seemed to detect a look of "How could you miss a straight away shot like that?" in her eyes.

Twenty minutes later, Jeff pointed to a flock of Canada geese that appeared as specks in the sky they were so far away. Again we hunkered down so only our eyes and our camouflaged hats were visible over the top of the blind. I gathered Josie close to me again, and we watched and waited as the geese slowly winged their way towards the blind. They were still a long, long way off but coming closer with each beat of their wings. Now I could hear their faint honking.

What happened next is the most memorable event of that excursion. Jeff pulled a goose call out of his pocket, took a deep breath and blew. The noise that came out of that call was unlike anything - mechanical or alive - that I have ever heard before or since that day in the blind on Lake Tichigan. It occurred to me that he had absolutely no idea of what his call sounded like, but there was no question in my mind that one thing it absolutely did not sound like was a Canada goose! Jeff kept calling, and the geese kept flying. They did not come within a hundred yards of our duck blind. After they passed, I jotted a note on the pad of paper asking him how he learned to call geese if he could not hear what the call sounded like. He told me that his dad worked with him, tuning the call, so that his calling sounded like a real goose. I could only guess that the call had somehow gotten terribly out of tune, perhaps from being bumped or dropped. Maybe it was the dampness that caused the tone to drastically change. Whatever the cause, it was not sounding like a goose! I scribbled him another note, suggesting that maybe the call got bumped and sounded just a little bit off.

As the sun began to dip low in the western sky, a couple of wigeon flew over the outer edge of the decoys, and we managed to knock them out of the sky. Josie finally got a chance to make a water retrieve that day. At quitting time, we loaded up the boat, gathered in the decoys, and headed back to the boat landing, now cloaked in shadows.

By the time we were back in the truck heading for home, it was pitch dark, so we rode again in silence. At one point on the drive, Jeff sneezed, and by force of habit, I turned and said, "God bless you." When I realized that he could not hear me, the thought of what had just happened struck me as hilarious, and I broke out in laughter. Jeff, of course, could not hear the laughter any more than he could hear the "God bless you," and that realization had me laughing all the harder. I do not know if he ever got his goose call re-tuned because that was the last time that Jeff and I had the chance to hunt ducks together. Either way, it was a very memorable day on the water.

21

CHUKAR CHALLENGE

EACH JANUARY, THE Hustisford Gun Club hosts a Chukar Challenge. At this event, a team of six hunters has four hours to hunt their respective field. Scattered throughout their field are fifty of these game birds - ten of them wearing colored bands on their legs. The object of the challenge, of course, is to shoot as many of the birds as possible in the field in the allotted time. The banded birds allow the shooters to earn tickets for the raffle at the Chukar Challenge Banquet which is held two weeks after the hunt. The hunt is spread out over two weekends, and each morning and each afternoon of each day of the hunt there are three fields each planted with fifty chukars. Over the course of the two weekends, there are six hundred chukars put out.

I arranged for a friend and owner of several German Wirehaired Pointers to join us this particular year. John also breeds Wirehairs, and I was interested in perhaps getting a puppy from an upcoming litter and wanted to see one of his dogs in action. John readily agreed to join us, and would bring one his wirehaired pointers, Gus. Another friend and his two sons-in-law would join my son Ben and me on this hunt.

The day of our hunt arrived, and we all met at the clubhouse in Hustisford. We ate pizza and drank soda with members of other teams before heading out into the fields. Once we arrived at our field, we decided that Larry, his relatives and his Brittany, Dixie, would start on the east end of the field which was the highest part of the area, while John, Ben and I - along with Josie and Gus - would begin our quest for chukars on the west end - along the creek that served as the boundary line between our field and the next. The two groups would eventually meet somewhere in the middle of the field.

We had only been in the field for about two minutes when Gus went on point. John flushed the bird, shot it, and Gus retrieved it in smart fashion. Nice looking dog. Only forty-nine birds to go. For the next hour or so, all of the dogs found birds, everybody got shooting, all of the dogs were retrieving birds. A good time was being had by all.

Members of the gun club drove four wheelers out to the fields during the hunt to collect the birds in five-gallon buckets so they could begin cleaning the birds for the hunters. Our six-person team met in the middle of our hunting area and began emptying our vests of the birds into two of the five-gallon pails that had been placed in the middle of the field for that purpose. Among the six of us, we had shot about thirty-five birds - eight of them sporting colored leg bands which we removed so we could exchange them for raffle tickets at the end of the hunt. We sat down to rest and to discuss our strategy for finishing the hunt while we waited for the buckets of birds to be collected.

As we were talking and exchanging tales from the morning's hunt, Josie took a few steps towards one of the buckets to have a little sniff of the birds. John's dog Gus, perhaps thinking that Josie was going to steal one of his birds, lunged at Josie's head, tearing open her left ear with one vicious bite! Josie let out a pitiful yelp. John was on Gus in a second, but the damage had been done. There was a two-inch rip in her ear but, surprisingly, her ear was bleeding very little. I thought back to the other time Josie had cut her ear ("Nicked Ear") and all of the blood that was lost during that episode. In addition to the fact that her torn ear was not bleeding, Josie also seemed not to be in much discomfort. She has always had a very high tolerance for pain, showing little concern for cuts and abrasions she has received during hunting outings over the years.

I told the other guys in the group that I was going to have to leave to get Josie to a vet in order to get her ear stitched up. John said that since there was so little bleeding, there was really no urgency to take care of it and that if I wanted to wait until the hunt was completed, we could drive over to his farm, which was only a few miles from Hustisford, and he would clean the wound and staple it shut for me. He said that he had done the same to his dogs over the years when they had sustained similar injuries. Going to John's farm did not seem like the prudent thing to do, but Josie did not seem to be bothered by the injury, and again, there was no bleeding from the cut. I told John that I was concerned about dirt getting into the wound. He replied that a washing with an antibiotic solution would take care of it and that it would not get infected. Since Josie seemed fine, I decided to go ahead with John's plan.

We hunted for another hour, picking up another six or seven birds before calling it quits and heading back to the trucks. I put Josie into her crate, carefully closing the door, ensuring her that she would be okay. We drove back to the clubhouse, dropped these last birds off at the cleaning station and went inside for a bowl of chili and a beverage while our birds were being cleaned.

A half hour later, with our cleaned and bagged chukars in hand, we headed out. John led the way towards his farm; Ben and I followed in our truck. Once at the farm, John put Gus into his kennel and went inside to get the first-aid supplies. He returned a few minutes later with a basin, a cloth and a veterinarian's stapler made for just such an injury. I gently took Josie out of her crate. While I held her close to me - one hand wrapped around her muzzle to prevent any adverse reactions, John cleaned up Josie's ear, then deftly closed the wound with seven staples.

Ten days later, with a newly acquired staple remover, I extracted the seven staples from Josie's ear. She has been as good as gold ever since!

22

Tower Hunt

I ARRANGED FOR a tower hunt at Cedar Hills Game Farm in Beaver Dam. For those of you who are not acquainted with a tower hunt, it is a whole different type of an affair than a typical field and forest hunt where the dog works out in front of the hunters and goes on point when she catches the scent of a hiding pheasant. With a tower hunt, there is, of course, a tower. The tower at Cedar Hills Game Farm is about forty feet high, approximately four stories, and similar in design and build to an observation tower that might be found in a state park. There are twelve shooting stations arranged in a circle around the tower, perhaps 40 or 50 yards distant. The shooting stations are configured similarly to the numbers on the face of a clock.

The pheasants are literally thrown into the air, one at a time, by a man in the tower, and as the bird takes flight, it makes for some pretty wild shooting action as the birds fly past the shooting stations where the gunners are located. It is very different kind of shooting because the birds are actually flying towards the shooters instead of away from them. By the time the birds are near the shooting stations on the perimeter, they may be 60 feet or more in the air and are flying very fast. After every five birds are launched, the gunners all rotate one station, thus ensuring every gunner has an equal opportunity at shooting over the course of the hunt.

There were seven hunters and two dogs on this particular hunt. My two sons, Ben and Jesse, along with my good friend, Larry, his two sons-in-law and his daughter, Caitlyn. Larry had his Brittany, Dixie, and I, of course, had my sweet girl, Josie.

Well, there were quite a few of the birds that managed to make it to safety after being released from the tower and flying past the perimeter of shooting stations. The nice thing about tower hunts is that after the "tower" part of the tower hunt is over, the hunters can bring their dogs out and have a "scratch bird" hunt for those birds. Thus it was, therefore, that Josie, Ben, Jesse and I struck off towards one section of the fields and woods, while Larry, Dixie, and his crew headed off to hunt another part of the property. We made plans to meet back at the parking lot in about an hour-and-a-half.

We had a general idea of where some of the birds flew to on the section of the property that we would be hunting, and we managed to pick up several of them as Josie had brought her "A" game and was doing a really good job of locating and pointing these second-chance birds. As the time remaining began to run out, we decided to hunt a small forest that led us back towards the parking lot. Ben and Jesse were on the outside edge of the woods, which was bordered by a cut corn field while I was further into the woods. The blanket of snow that covered the ground made it pretty easy to catch sight of their blaze-orange hats and vests through the trees. The same blanket of white, however, had continually caused Josie's Swiss bell to fall silent as it became packed with snow and had to be cleaned out in order for me to keep track of her. But, for the most part, we were able to keep pretty close tabs on her. The boys and I would often call back and forth to each other to be sure we knew where each other - and the dog - were at all times.

Some moments had gone by since I had seen Josie, and without her tinkling bell, it was more difficult to know exactly where she was just then. I yelled across to the guys to see if Josie was with them. No, they thought she was with me, as they had not seen her for four or five minutes, about the length of time since I had seen her as well. We quickly determined that we would need to backtrack to find her. So back we went. About a hundred yards back, we caught sight of Josie. She was locked up on point, right on the edge of the cut corn, standing like a statue. Her gaze was fixed on a tangle of brush, about ten feet from where she stood. We determined that she must have been on point for at least the last ten minutes while the three of us moved through the trees, totally unaware of the fact that she had located a bird!

I wondered what was going through her head as I moved up alongside her and softly told her to "Whoa, girl, whoa." Probably something like, "What do you think I've been doing for the last ten minutes?!" We all three got into position for a shot when the bird flushed. I moved in and kicked at the tangle of brush where her quivering nose was pointed. With a flurry of feathers and that distinctive cackling, a majestic rooster rocketed skyward, streaking out above the cut corn field. I missed completely with the first shot and frantically ejected the spent shell and prepared for a second shot which dislodged a few feathers, but the bird kept gaining altitude. Both Ben and Jesse let fly and the rooster tumbled to the ground landing with a soft thud in the white, fluffy snow. A moment later Josie came trotting back to us, holding her ring-necked prize proudly in her soft mouth. A splendid finish to a great day of hunting!

23

The Nose Knows

By the time Josie reached her twelfth season of hunting, she had slowed down considerably compared to her younger days when she exhibited both speed and range. She had been hit by the car when she was only a year old, and she had ACL repairs on both of her back legs. Arthritis had crept into her back and her joints. Her hearing had begun to deteriorate. Gray was now her predominant color - no longer brown. But her nose and her eyes were still good, and she had the heart of a champion. Over the past few years, I had been struck by the similarities between Josie and my father, Earl, who was now eighty-eight years old, as they both were showing their old age. Dad, like Josie, had slowed considerably, but he was also compromised by Alzheimer's Disease which was robbing him of his memory. Dad's hearing had begun to fade, and he now wore hearing aids in both ears. Also like Josie, there were so many precious memories of wonderful hunting adventures with Dad while I was growing up, though most of those reminiscences were tied to duck hunting on Green Bay. The circle of life can only end in dying. Rather than dwelling on what was to come, I relished fond memories of days gone by.

So it was in her twelfth season, that I found myself out at the Ozaukee County Gun Club with my beloved Josie, who was as anxious as ever to get the hunt under way. This particular morning, we would be joined by two other members of the club and their dogs. Pat was there with Rocky, his German Shorthair and a real speed demon. Rocky had one speed - wide open! He was also a far-running dog. Roger was with us again, along with his English Setter, Belle, who was also a hard-charging, fast-moving pooch. So the dogs were a study in contrast - the two younger dogs who flew across the field, and Josie, who plodded along, taking her time. She took more of a "slow but sure wins the race" kind of approach to hunting.

The snow was deep that day, which made it even more difficult for my old girl to maneuver in the field. The three hunters set out together this day along with the three dogs. Belle and Rocky took off like rockets when they were released into the field while Josie - her little tail wagging constantly - trotted out into the field, smelling the smells and seeing the sights. After thirty minutes, Belle and Rocky each put up two birds that their owners had cleanly killed with one shot each. We decided to make one last swing and then head back to the clubhouse. Rocky and Belle continued their far ranging zig-zagging and criss-crossing. Josie continued her methodical, steady work still searching for her first bird of the day. As she neared a small rise at the edge of the woods, Josie became quite birdy - sniffing more intently, circling around the same area a few times, tail wagging even faster, head only a couple of inches off the deep snow. I called over to the other guys that Josie might be onto something. They replied that both of the other dogs had been through that area a couple of times already so it might just be old scent from a previous bird that Josie was smelling. "I don't know, guys. She likes something here." I decided to hang back with Josie as she continued to work a small patch while Pat and Roger began to work their way back to the clubhouse.

After five more minutes of covering the same thirty feet, Josie locked up, her nose pointing at the side of a big snowbank devoid of any cover. There was no grass, no brush, no nothing. But Josie remained staunchly on point. Trusting my dog's nose more than my own eyes, I began to shuffle through the snow bank in a back-and-forth pattern covering the entire snow bank, one square foot at a time. Nothing. Still Josie remained on point. So I began a second pass through the same thirty feet of snow - back and forth. As I was about to call Josie off and call it a day, a rooster burst from the snow bank so close I could have grabbed it with my hands had I not been so surprised that I stumbled backwards. Cackling wildly in protest that his hiding place had been disturbed, the long tail quickly gained altitude. The first shot from my trusty 12 gauge knocked a few feathers from him, but he kept flying. The second shot seemed to miss completely. As I drew a bead for my third and final shot, I thought about how hard Josie had worked for this bird, I hoped that I could bring him down. As I squeezed the trigger, I could see that I found my mark. While not a lethal hit, the rooster started coming down in a long slow glide. The pheasant came down some seventy-five yards from where I stood. I knew that it was not dead, but I did not think it could run very fast or very far in the deep, fluffy snow. With her eyes locked onto her prize, Josie took off at the shot. Three minutes had passed - although it seemed like thirty - when I saw Josie plowing her way back to me with the rooster held firmly in her soft mouth. It was a beautiful sight - her old gray fuzzy face full of snow and full of rooster. What a perfect ending to a great day in the field. The nose knows.

Epilogue

As *The Gospel According to Josie* goes to print, Josie is well into her fourteenth year. Her beautiful brown eyes are beginning to cloud a little. She has lost some of her hearing. She has arthritis in her back and legs. You can feel her spine and ribs when you pet her. Her muzzle is mostly gray. She spends much of her day taking naps.

But we still take our morning walks together every day. She still has to take one lap around the dining room table before she will let me put the collar on her before we begin our walks. Every night I am awakened several times to the clicking of her toenails on the hallway tiles as she walks down to our bedroom to peer in to make sure I'm still there. Satisfied, she will pad back to her bed in the dining room and go back to sleep, only to repeat the process a few hours later. She still knows no greater joy than to be near me, to spend time with me.

Time will tell what the upcoming hunting season will bring. Hopefully, Josie will be able to work the fields for an hour or so before tiring. If so, wonderful. If not, so be it. The cherished memories of the adventures we have shared over the years will be carried in my heart for the rest of my days. Happy hunting.

PJS

About the Author

P.J. Sanders is a retired teacher, counselor, and elementary school principal.

He lives with his wife, Cindy, and his dog, Josie, in Menomonee Falls, Wisconsin. Josie came into Sanders's life after his first dog was shot and killed by another hunter in North Dakota.